Invest Like a Guru

Invest Like a Guru

HOW TO GENERATE HIGHER RETURNS
AT REDUCED RISK WITH VALUE
INVESTING

Charlie Tian, Ph.D.

WILEY

Library of Congress Cataloging-in-Publication Data is Available:

ISBN 978-1-119-36236-4 (Hardcover)
ISBN 978-1-119-36242-5 (ePDF)
ISBN 978-1-119-36240-1 (ePub)

Cover Design: Wiley
Cover Images: texture © gaffera/Getty Images, Inc.; icon © RENGraphic/Getty Images, Inc.

Printed in the United States of America

SKY10087872_101524

To my parents, wife, and children

Contents

Acknowledgments

I want to thank Lei, my wife, for the strength and inspiration she gives me daily. Thanks to my parents for their encouragement and trust throughout my life. Thanks to my son, Charles, who programmed the first version of GuruFocus DCF Calculator when he was 12; my daughter Alice, whose soccer games have been my biggest joy; and my little son, Matthew, who has brought me so much fun and happiness.

I also want to thank Don Li, Holly LaFon, David Goodloe, Vera Yuan, and many others at GuruFocus. They have transformed Guru-Focus from good to great.

Thanks to the 300,000 GuruFocus users and 18,000+ subscribers for their constant feedback and suggestions over the past 12 years. They have helped us make GuruFocus.com a better website.

I cannot express enough appreciation to Warren Buffett and Peter Lynch, although they will probably never know this. Their teaching has unleashed my full potential and led me to reach new heights in life. I am grateful to the United States of America. This great land has given me the opportunity to fulfill my dreams. I also give thanks to my alma mater, Peking University. The rigorous training I received during my 11 years there prepared me for quick learning across different fields.

I also want to thank the Gurus who gave me the opportunities to speak with them and interview them over the years. These Gurus include Prem Watsa of Fairfax Financial, Francis Chou of Chou Associates, Joel Greenblatt of Gotham Funds, Tom Russo of Gardner and Russo, Don Yacktman and Jason Subotky of Yacktman Asset Management, Jeff Auxier of Auxier Capital, Tom Gayer of Markel Corp., and many others.

Thanks to Erin McKnight, Jennifer Afflerbach, who has edited my writing, and my friends, LeAnn Chen and Wenhua Di, for their comments and suggestions.

Introduction

Before I came to the United States, I'd never envisioned being caught up in a stock market mania that would drastically alter my career and completely change my life. I loved physics, which I had studied for many years, and assumed I would become a physics professor someday. I'd never had anything to do with the stock market.

The summer of 1998 was hot, even for Texas. I came to work for Texas A&M University in an equally "hot" field in the physics department: fiber optics and lasers. This was during the momentous expansion of the Internet and the telecommunication industry, and everything related to the technological boom was hot, everything related to fiber optics was hot!

By then, I already had my PhD in physics in the field of lasers and optics from Peking University. I was excited to be working in a field that seemed to hold unlimited potential, and I found that people like me were in strong demand. In less than two years I was recruited by a fiber optical communications company that would soon go public. Business was booming. The company had dramatically expanded its office space and hired hundreds of additional engineers. The benefit that most attracted people to work for this particular company was its stock option offering. I had no idea what stock options were—I just knew that they would be worth a lot of money!

Everyone was talking about stocks and stock options. *It sounds like fun! And it can make me money! I need to buy stocks,* I told myself. *I need to buy fiber optics stocks!*

I felt that I had an edge. After all, I had worked with lasers and fiber optics for many years. I had published many research papers and would ultimately be awarded 32 patents in the field. I knew exactly how fiber optics worked.

I also knew the fiber optics companies. I used their products in my work, and demand for them was tremendous. Internet traffic was booming and the need for Internet capacity and fiber optics networks was expected to grow 1,000 percent a year. Companies like Global Crossing were laying fiber across oceans. WorldCom was hosting an exciting Terabyte Challenge, which would squeeze a terabyte per second of bandwidth into a single optical fiber. The demand for fiber network capacity, it seemed, would grow exponentially, forever.

In a trillion-dollar market, no one could lose, analysts wrote. The stocks of these fiber optics companies would double in three months, and that was true for every fiber optics company that was going public.

I started my shopping spree. In 2000, I bought the stocks of fiber optics companies New Focus, Oplink, and Corning. Corning, the old dog that learned a new trick in fiber optics, was making the optical fiber cable used in fiber networks. It didn't disappoint me, quickly doubling and then some. Corning was doing so well in fact that the stock went on a 3:1 split. It was fun!

But, I would later realize, I was lucky I didn't have much money to buy stocks with back then.

The Bloodbath

The party didn't last very long—and I'd arrived late.

Without my realizing it, things were turning sour with my employer. By the end of 2000, the company was already quietly laying off contractors and temporary workers. It turned out that our biggest customers, WorldCom and Global Crossing, were having their own problems and had stopped buying equipment.

Then 9/11 hit and everything came to a grinding halt. My company had lost 80 percent of its sales from the previous year, and WorldCom was on the verge of bankruptcy. All new product development had ceased, and my company was now ruthlessly laying people off. In less than two years the company had lost more than 75 percent of its employees and was itself on life support. The people who were still there, including myself, felt lucky just to have a job. No one talked about stock options any longer. The company's initial public offering (IPO) plan had long since been shelved, permanently.

So, what happened to my fiber optics stocks? The chart below illustrates the stock prices of Corning from January 2000 to the end of 2002. I bought the stock in January 2000 at around $40 a share (split-adjusted). In about nine months, it almost tripled—going all

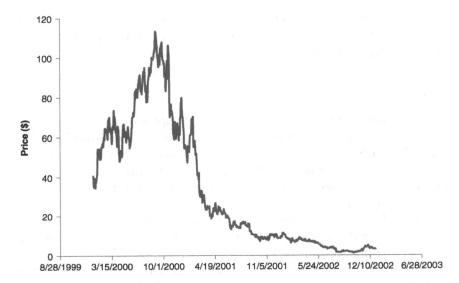

Figure I.1   Price Chart of Corning

the way up to $110. Then it started its decline. For a while I didn't budge, as I still had a sizable gain. Of course, it never went straight down. It fluctuated. And these fluctuations gave me hope. *It will come back*, I kept telling myself. Then, in 2001, as the bad news about the telecom industry flooded in, the falling accelerated. By mid-2001, I had lost half of my investment in the stock. I continued to ride the rollercoaster all the way to the bottom.

My Oplink stock fared worse. I bought at the IPO, thinking it would double in three months, as Wall Street predicted. It never did. The price of Oplink almost never went above its IPO price. Of course, it, too, fluctuated and gave me hope.

It was painful to look at the balance of my brokerage account, so I stopped checking. Instead, I started reading Peter Lynch's *Beating the Street*.[1] I gradually realized that those fiber optics stocks were terrible investments for me to make, so in the fourth quarter of 2002, I threw in the towel and sold everything at more than a 90 percent loss—right when the prices bottomed and they actually became much better investments, as I will explain in Chapter 2.

It took some 15 years for the Nasdaq index to return to where it had been at its 2000 peak. As of June 2016, and even after so many years, the Dow Jones U.S. Telecommunications Index is just above 50 percent of its 2000 apex.

An industry went from boom to bust. A bubble burst. As I would later learn, this kind of boom–bust cycle has been repeated many times throughout history.

The Bubbles

In his book, *A Short History of Financial Euphoria*,[2] economics professor John Kenneth Galbraith discusses all the speculative bubbles since the early 1600s. He argues that financial memory is "notoriously short" and defines bubbles as created by human speculation when there is something new and there is an abundant amount of money from leverage.

Mark Twain said: "History does not repeat itself, but it rhymes." It turns out that the fiber optics bubble was just another "rhyme" of bubbles that have come before.

The first recorded economic bubble was the Dutch tulip mania in the late 1630s. At its peak, any tulip bulb could fetch a price equivalent to many years of earnings of a skilled worker. People were selling land and houses to speculate in the tulip market. Another phenomenal historical bubble involves the stock of the South Sea Company. The company was established in the early eighteenth century and was granted a monopoly on trade in South Sea in exchange for assuming England's war debt. Investors loved the appeal of the monopoly, and the company's stock price began to rise. Just as with any bubble, high prices drove the price ever higher, and even Sir Isaac Newton wasn't immune to the speculation. In 1720, Newton invested a meager sum in South Sea; a few months later, he had tripled his investment and therefore sold his position. But the stock price continued to rise at an even faster pace. Newton came to regret the sale as he watched his friends quickly become rich, so he went all-in at three times the price he had sold for. The price did continue to increase for a time, but then it collapsed. Newton sold his position at a great loss at the end of 1720. The entire drama had lasted less than a year, and Newton lost £20,000, which constituted his life savings.

Even Newton, one of the smartest people in all of history, couldn't escape the destruction caused by the bubble. He created the entire theory of classical physics with the inspiration of being hit on the head by an apple, but he couldn't overcome the emotions of greed and fear. He later wrote: "I can calculate the movement of stars, but not the madness of men."[3]

It was amusing to learn that the founding father of the field of my academic study had lost so much money in a stock bubble, just like me. Not that it made me feel any better.

The fiber optics bubble was like all past bubbles in terms of the associated greed for something new and the abundance of money and leverage. As in prior bubbles, speculation soared as a result of the Internet explosion, which made people expect that the demand for fiber optics networks would also explode and thus a significant amount of money could be made building fiber optical networks. Companies like WorldCom and Global Crossing were borrowing money to build optical networks and were laying fiber everywhere, which inflated the demand for optical network equipment. For equipment suppliers like Nortel and Alcatel, and my former employer, business was booming. They invested heavily in product development and manufacturing capacities, which further drove the demand for optical components. As a result, hundreds of optical component companies popped up in Silicon Valley.

Funds were unlimited. A PowerPoint presentation could land you tens of millions in investment dollars and get your startup going. When I attended the Optical Fiber Communication Conference in early 2001, mountains of free pens greeted me. You could grab as many as you wanted! Companies were giving out all kinds of fancy toys to anyone who passed their booth. This was in March 2001. The Nasdaq index had already lost more than 60 percent from its peak a year before, but the fiber optics companies were still going crazy.

Unlike the dot-com companies that had no revenue, fiber optics companies did. Oplink had $131 million in revenue for 2001, although it lost $25 million on that. But the demand for bandwidth didn't grow fast enough. The overinvestment and the innovations in telecom technology by people like me created far more capacity than the Internet traffic needed. The overcapacity and overbuilt infrastructure drove the cost of data transmission dramatically lower. We could now squeeze much more capacity into a single fiber, and there were too many fibers. The price of data traffic collapsed— 97 percent of the fiber laid was dark. WorldCom and Global Crossing found that they couldn't service their debt and were forced into bankruptcy. The bottom fell out of the entire industry. By 2002, Oplink's revenue had dropped to $37 million, and $75 million was lost on that. My former employer lost more than 80 percent of its own revenue, and in the years that followed, many of the telecom equipment companies went belly up. The industry never recovered, much like the tulip bulb market.

You would think that humankind would learn from past bubbles, but the creation of bubbles never stopped. There are four recurring types of participants during the expansion phase of bubbles:

1. *The average folks:* These are the people who are excited about the new idea and are also relatively new to the market. They think they are onto something and because their friends and neighbors are getting rich, they, too, should jump in. I was one of them. So was Sir Isaac Newton. Widely recognized as the smartest person alive during his time, Newton was just an average guy when it came to the stock market.

2. *The smart ones:* These are the people who recognize that something is wrong, yet think they can figure out when the bubble will burst—they will ride all the way to the peak, but get out before everyone else. As Warren Buffett joked in his 2007 shareholder letter, after the burst of the dot-com bubble in the early 2000s, Silicon Valley had a popular bumper sticker that read: *Please, God, Just One More Bubble.* Before long, they got one. This time in housing, and we all know how that ended.[4]

3. *The short sellers:* These are the people who recognize that things are wrong and that what is happening is not sustainable. Stocks are overpriced. So they short the stocks by borrowing the shares and selling them, hoping to buy the shares back at a much lower price or not to buy back at all if the company goes bankrupt. But then their pain begins. The stocks continue to go up and short sellers are losing more and more money. Just as economist John Keynes pointed out, "Markets can remain irrational a lot longer than you and I can remain solvent." This happened to one of the most celebrated investors, George Soros, the man who broke the Bank of England. During the beginning of 1999, Soros's fund was betting big against Internet stocks. He saw the bubble taking shape and knew that the Internet craze would end badly. But as the craze kept gathering force, his fund lost 20 percent by the middle of 1999. Though he knew that the Internet bubble would burst, he bought the borrowed shares back and closed his short positions. That wasn't enough.

Under performance pressure, he turned against what he knew—which was the right thing to do—and became the next type of bubble participant: the forced buyer.

4. *The forced buyers:* These are the professional investors who are forced to participate in a bubble, mostly under pressure to deliver short-term gains. Not getting involved in the Next Big Thing would make them look outdated, and they face losing jobs or clients. After closing his short positions in Internet stocks, and feeling he couldn't buy those stocks himself, George Soros hired someone to do it for him. His portfolio was then filled with the Internet stocks he hated. Not only that, but the new guy was now selling short the old-economy stocks. It worked. By the end of 1999, Soros saw his fund come all the way back to finish 1999 up 35 percent. The problem was that in another few months, Soros's prediction of the burst of the Internet bubble came true, and he found himself turned in the wrong direction again.

Those people who recognized the bubble and decided to stay out and instead wait for opportunities were (and are) the truly smart investors. But their lives weren't necessarily any easier, especially if they were managing someone else's money. Warren Buffett was considered "to have lost his magic touch."[5] Hedge fund legend Julian Robertson saw his fund in a downward spiral as investors withdrew in response to his shunning of Internet stocks; he closed his fund just as the bubble started to burst. Donald Yacktman, one of the most rational value investors, lost more than 90 percent of the fund's assets to redemptions. The fund's board of directors wanted him out, and only a proxy fight helped him remain in the fund that bears his name. Steven Romick, the excellent young manager of FPA Crescent Fund, was luckier. Though 85 percent of the fund was redeemed, the remaining 15 percent of shareholders "forgot they had invested in the fund," he assumed, and he kept his job.[6]

Those who stick to what they believe through the tough times are my true investment Gurus. In the years that followed the Internet and fiber optics bubbles, I read everything these stock market masters wrote. Their teachings have completely changed the way I think about business and investing and have made me a better investor.

GuruFocus.com

I don't recall how I found out about Peter Lynch, but it was through Lynch's books[7] that I learned about Warren Buffett and his mentor, Ben Graham. I then read all of Buffett's shareholder and partnership letters from the past 40 years. Upon finishing these letters, I was exhausted. I felt like a hungry man who had enjoyed the first complete meal of his life. I thought, *This is the right way to invest!*

I realized that successful investing is about knowledge and hard work. It is a lifelong learning process—there is no other secret. Only through learning can you build confidence in your investment decision making. Knowledge and confidence help you to think rationally and independently, especially during market panics and euphoria—when rational and independent thinking is most needed. The good news is that if you learn, you *will* get better.

I started GuruFocus during the Christmas holiday of 2004 to share what I'd learned. Over the course of its existence, I have probably learned more from GuruFocus users than they have from me. I cannot sufficiently describe my enjoyment. I certainly worked hard. I would get up at 4 A.M., after only three hours of sleep, work four hours until 8 A.M., eat some breakfast, then go to my full-time job in fiber optics. I would come back home at 6 P.M. and immediately go back to work on GuruFocus. I loved weekends and holidays because I could work without stopping.

In 2007, I quit my full-time job and put all my time and effort into the website. I also gradually built a team of software developers, editors, and data analysts to work on GuruFocus. We developed many screening tools and added a lot of data in the areas of Guru portfolios, insiders, industry profile, and company financials. I built these screeners and valuation tools initially for my own investing. We continue to improve them in response to feedback from our knowledgeable users. These tools are now the only ones I use in my investment decision-making process.

In the meantime, I continue to invest in the stock market with my own money, making mistakes and learning from them along the way. I believe that I have become a much better investor. I feel that I have many lessons and much experience to share with my children; I hope that they don't make similar mistakes. Though they may not work in the investing field in the future, I want to guide them in the right direction when managing their own money—which is why I wrote this book. I hope that even people without much prior knowledge in investing can benefit from it.

This book is divided into three sections. The first focuses on where to find the companies that may generate higher returns with smaller risk. The second deals with how to evaluate these companies, how to find possible problems with them, and how to avoid mistakes. The third further discusses stock valuations, general market valuations, and returns. Many easy-to-follow case studies and real examples are used throughout the book.

CHAPTER 1

The Gurus

"Those who keep learning will keep rising in life."

—Charlie Munger[1]

The painful experience I had in the stock market during the dot-com bubble made me realize that I knew nothing about stocks. So, I started to learn. In the years that followed, I was reading everything I could find from some of the best investors. I read their books, their quarterly or annual shareholder letters, and any articles about them I could locate. I looked at their portfolios for investment ideas. And, in 2004, I started GuruFocus.com to share what I had learned. Then I learned even more, as many of the investors came to the website to share what *they* had learned.

I discovered that investing can be learned. I discovered that there is no trick to becoming a better investor. You simply need to learn, learn from the best, and learn from mistakes—mistakes of others, but mostly your own. And you need to work really hard.

The Gurus who had the most impact on me and my investing philosophy are Peter Lynch, Warren Buffett, Donald Yacktman, and Howard Marks. Lynch, Buffett, and Yacktman taught me how to think about business, companies, and their stocks. Marks made a great impression on me regarding how to think about market cycles and risks. What follows in this chapter are the important points that I gleaned from these Gurus.

Peter Lynch

Peter Lynch is the Guru from whom I learned the most about stock picking. The legendary mutual fund manager of the 1980s at Fidelity invested in thousands of companies and generated an annualized average return of 29 percent a year for 13 years. His bestselling books, *Beating the Street*[2] and *One Up on Wall Street*,[3] are the first books I read, and they helped me build the foundation for my investing knowledge. I read these books over and over and still learn something from them. I will use some of Lynch's quotes to explain the key factors in his investing.

"Earnings, Earnings, Earnings"

A company's earnings and its stock price relative to earnings are by far the most important factors in deciding if the stock is a good investment. Though stock prices can be affected by daily headlines about the Federal Reserve, the unemployment rate, the weekly jobs report, or what's going on in Europe, over the long term, the noise from the news is canceled out. As Lynch wrote:[4]

> People may wonder what the Japanese are doing and what the Koreans are doing, but ultimately the earnings will decide the fate of a stock. People may bet the hourly wiggles in the market, but it's the earnings that waggle the wiggles, long-term.

Lynch places all companies in six categories:

1. Fast growers
2. The stalwarts
3. Slow growers
4. Cyclicals
5. Turnarounds
6. Asset plays

Excluding the last category, asset plays, the companies are categorized based on what their earnings do. A fast grower can grow its earnings at above 20 percent a year. The stalwarts can grow at above 10 percent a year. The slow grower grows its earnings at single digits a year. Cyclicals are obviously the companies that have cyclical earnings. Turnarounds are those that have just stopped losing money and have started to generate earnings.

To Lynch, a company's earnings, earnings growth, and the earnings related to valuation ratios are the first things to look at before you consider a company further, unless you know it is an asset play. You can find all this information in a company's income statement. After I learned this, I went back to check the earnings of the fiber optics companies I bought. This was what I found in the 2001 annual report of Oplink:[5]

> We have incurred significant losses since our inception in 1995 and expect to incur losses in the future. We incurred net losses of $80.4 million, $24.9 million and $3.5 million for the fiscal years ended June 30, 2001, 2000 and 1999, respectively.

So, the company had been losing money all that time and was expected to lose more in the future—how *could* its stock do well? By simply looking at the earnings, investors like myself would not have bought stocks like Oplink and could have avoided a monumental mistake.

I immediately included this in my investing practice. In the plaza behind the community where I lived were a Starbucks and a Blockbuster. The two stores were next to each other. I was deciding, between them, which stock to buy. It was October 2001, and I went to visit the stores many times to observe their operations and traffic as part of my research, as suggested by Lynch. I couldn't tell the difference just by visiting the stores, however. Both stores seemed to have decent traffic, which was confirmed by pretty good sales numbers. I definitely didn't foresee that one day Blockbuster would be killed by Netflix. What made the difference is Lynch's "earnings, earnings, earnings." Starbucks has always been profitable and was growing its earnings at more than 30 percent a year, whereas Blockbuster was losing money four out of five years from 1996 to 2000. In addition, Starbucks had almost no debt and a much stronger balance sheet than Blockbuster.

The decision became simple, and I bought Starbucks in October 2001. I sold it in March 2003 for a 65 percent gain. As I learned more, I realized that Starbucks is a fast grower—which makes me wish I'd never sold.

Since earnings are the most important measure of a company's profitability, the companies that have higher profit margins beat those with lower profit margins. The ones with increasing profit margins beat the companies with declining margins; therefore, unsurprisingly, Lynch prefers companies with higher margins to those with lower margins.[6]

"Companies That Have No Debt Can't Go Bankrupt"

If earnings, earnings, earnings are the measure of a company's profitability, the above quote from Lynch references the financial strength of a company, which is reflected on the company's balance sheet.

A company's debt level is the most important factor when measuring its financial strength. A company goes bankrupt if it cannot service or repay its debt, even if it may have a lot of valuable assets. A company's debt level is closely related to the nature of the business and its operations. For businesses that don't need a lot of capital to grow, the chance of accumulating a large debt load is small. One such company is Moody's. The credit rating agency is a favorite holding of Buffett. Some companies need a lot of capital investment in their operations and are therefore considered capital-intensive and asset heavy, such as mining companies and utilities.

According to the debt loads of different companies, we can categorize them into four levels (A–D):

A. No debt

This type of company has no debt or minimal debt. One example is Chipotle Mexican Grill. Chipotle has grown its earnings at 30 percent a year without incurring any debt. These are the related balance sheet items of Chipotle over the past five years (all numbers in millions):

Fiscal Period	Dec2011	Dec2012	Dec2013	Dec2014	Dec2015
Cash, Cash Equivalents, Marketable Securities	456	472	578	758	663
Current Portion of Long-Term Debt	0.133	0	0	0	0
Long-Term Debt	3.5	0	0	0	0

A large portion of Chipotle's growth is from expanding into new markets. A major risk for fast growers like Chipotle is expanding too fast and then needing to borrow money to fund the growth. This clearly wasn't the case for Chipotle. If bought at a reasonable price, which I will discuss in Chapter 5, this stock's investment risk is low.

B. Some debt, but easily serviced by existing cash or operating cash flow

Most companies have some level of debt on their balance sheet. A company may have a debt level that is less than its cash level and can be paid off easily, for instance, Agilent Technologies, the maker of test and measurement equipment. These are the related items from its balance sheet and income statement; again, all numbers are in millions:

Fiscal Year	2006	2007	2008	2009	2010	2011	2012	2013	2014	2015
Cash	2262	1826	1429	2493	2649	3527	2351	2675	2218	2003
Current Portion of Long-Term Debt	0	0	0	1	1501	253	250	0	0	0
Long-Term Debt	1500	2087	2125	2904	2190	1932	2112	2699	1663	1655
Revenue	4973	5420	5774	4481	5444	6615	6858	6782	6981	4038
Operating Income	464	584	795	47	566	1071	1119	951	831	522
Net Interest Income	109	81	–10	–59	–76	–72	–92	–100	–104	–59

Agilent does have debt. In fact, as of October 2015, it had $1.65 billion of debt. But it also has more than $2 billion in cash. In principle, it can pay off all its debt outright with the cash in the bank. The company's past operating results further confirm that it is in a strong financial position. We can see that even during the economic recession in 2008 and 2009, the company could easily service its debt with its operating income. An investor should feel comfortable that the company can manage its debt in the future.

Some companies may not have enough cash to pay off their debt outright, but their operating cash flow can service their debt very comfortably. An example of such a company is AutoZone:

Fiscal Year	2006	2007	2008	2009	2010	2011	2012	2013	2014	2015
Cash	92	87	242	93	98	98	103	142	124	175
Current Portion of Long-Term Debt	0	16	0	0	48	34	80	206	217	41
Long-Term Debt	1857	1936	2250	2727	2882	3318	3718	4013	4142	4625
Revenue	5948	6170	6523	6817	7363	8073	8604	9148	9475	10187
Operating Income	1010	1055	1124	1176	1319	1495	1629	1773	1830	1953
Net Interest Income	−108	−119	−117	−142	−159	−171	−176	−185	−168	−150

AutoZone has always had much more debt than cash, but the company could easily service its debt, as its operating income is many times higher than the interest payment on its debt, during good times and bad. Although it is not a balance sheet that an investor should aim to have, it seems unnecessary to worry about the financial stability of the company.

Closer examination reveals that the company has been using the cash flow generated from operations to buy back shares, which reduced the company's cash balance.

C. Low interest coverage

While I like to eat Dunkin' Donuts, I don't like the company's balance sheet. The company has far more debt than cash. Although the same is true for AutoZone, Dunkin's interest payment on its debt is a much higher percentage of its operating income. During difficult times like in 2009, the interest payment consumed more than half of its operating income.

These are related items from Dunkin's balance sheet and income statement:

Fiscal Year	2009	2010	2011	2012	2013	2014	2015
Cash	0	134	247	253	257	208	260
Current Portion of Long-Term Debt	0	13	15	27	5	4	26
Long-Term Debt	0	1852	1458	1831	1826	1803	2428
Revenue	538	577	628	658	714	749	811
Operating Income	185	194	205	239	305	339	320
Net Interest Income	–115	–113	–104	–73	–80	–68	–96

For starters, a company's interest coverage is defined as the ratio of its operating income over its interest expense on its debt. In Dunkin's case, for fiscal year 2015, it had $320 million in operating income, but $96 million in interest expense. Therefore, the interest coverage is $320/96 = 3.3$.

A cautious investor should not feel comfortable holding the stock of companies with this kind of balance sheet. An interest coverage higher than 10 means that the operating income is more than ten times the interest payment on the debt, which indicates that the company can easily service its debt. If another recession hits or if interest rates go up, at least one of which will occur sooner or later, the earnings of Dunkin' will dramatically decrease. In the worst case, the company may even have a hard time servicing its debt.

Dunkin' Donuts is an example of a company with a weak balance sheet and relatively poor financial strength.

D. Cannot service its debt

Companies with even worse balance sheets cannot pass the test of bad times and are on their way to bankruptcy or have already gone bankrupt. An example of such a company is SandRidge Energy. The company always had a full load of debt on its balance sheet and far less cash. This is a similar situation to AutoZone, but SandRidge Energy barely generated enough operating income to service its interest payment for its debt even during good times, when the oil price was at an all-time high. After oil prices collapsed in 2015, the company was losing a major amount of money with operations and had no way to service its debt. It filed for bankruptcy in May 2016.

Fiscal Year	2006	2007	2008	2009	2010	2011	2012	2013	2014	2015
Cash	39	63	1	8	6	208	310	815	181	436
Current Portion of Long-Term Debt	26	15	17	12	7	1	0	0	0	0
Long-Term Debt	1041	1052	2359	2581	2902	2826	4301	3195	3195	3632
Revenue	388	677	1182	591	932	1415	2731	1983	1559	769
Operating Income	37	187	–1338	–1605	–7	429	325	–169	590	–4643
Net Interest Income	–16	–112	–143	–185	–247	–237	–303	–270	–244	–321

Investors should always avoid companies that have too much debt. SandRidge was a company with $12 billion of market cap at its peak, but SandRidge shareholders could have avoided their losses if they had taken a look at its balance sheet and its earnings, earnings, and earnings! I only feel comfortable investing in a company if its operating income covers at least ten times the interest payment on its debt, through good times and bad.

Again, as Lynch said, companies that have no debt can't go bankrupt. Oplink, the little fiber optics company whose stock I bought during the tech bubble, lost money nine out of the first ten years after it went public (2000–2009). The company went through two recessions but survived both and did so simply because it didn't have debt. Oplink was later acquired by Koch Optics for $445 million. At the time of acquisition, the company had $40 million in cash and no debt. The revenue had grown to $207 million a year, but the company was still barely profitable. The bigger players in the telecom market, such as Nortel, WorldCom, and Global Crossing, are long gone and forgotten. Too much debt!

A company's debt level is closely related to the nature of the business and its operations—some businesses are just better businesses. This leads to Lynch's third point:

"Go for a Business That Any Idiot Can Run"

The complete quote is:

> Go for a business that any idiot can run—because sooner or later any idiot probably is going to be running it.[7]

There are two types of companies that any idiot can run. One has a simple product and simple operations. The growth plan is to sell more of what it makes and repeat what it has done in more places. There is no deep insight and knowledge needed to make product and business decisions. In Lynch's own words from *One Up on Wall Street*:[8]

> Getting the story on a company is a lot easier if you understand the basic business. That's why I'd rather invest in panty hose than in communications satellites, or in motel chains than in fiber optics. The simpler it is, the better I like it. When somebody says, "Any idiot could run this joint," that's a plus as far as I'm concerned, because sooner or later any idiot probably is going to be running it.

Consider Research-In-Motion, now BlackBerry, which had nearly 50 percent of the smartphone market in the United States in 2008: A few wrong product decisions and slow moves wiped out almost all of its market share. It took more than a genius to compete against companies like Apple and Google, which are run by geniuses, too.

Another type of business that any idiot can run is the kind where strong competitive advantages protect it from management missteps and leave plenty of time for the company to correct its mistakes. McDonald's made plenty of mistakes, such as being slow to react to customers' changing tastes and needs and featuring a huge menu, which led to a worse customer experience. For the three years from 2013 through 2015, the company had declining same-store sales, one of the most important indicators of restaurant operations. It went through many CEOs in a few short years and seemed to have done everything wrong. Then, McDonald's introduced all-day breakfast in October 2015 and made adjustments to its food prep. The same-store sales had surged by January 2016, and the stock rallied to an all-time high. Back in 2007, both Research-In-Motion and McDonald's had about $60 billion in market cap. The mistakes made by Research-In-Motion wiped out more than 90 percent of its total market value while McDonald's market cap has grown to more than $100 billion.

Again consider Moody's, one of Buffett's favorite holdings. The rating agency enjoys a duopoly with S&P Global in the credit and bond rating markets. During the housing bubble of the mid-2000s, the company abused its power as a rating agency and assigned AAA ratings to the mortgage-backed securities that were actually very risky. The company was partially responsible for the housing crisis, and that cost it its credibility. Following the housing crisis, government agencies across the United States and Europe set up regulations to reduce the power of Moody's and S&P Global by pushing bond issuers to their smaller competitors, but this move didn't do much to the market share of Moody's. The company now has record sales and near-record profits. Its stock has also made new highs.

Therefore, if everything else is equal, buy the company that can grow by copying what it is doing in more places, or buy the ones that are protected from competition by their strong competitive advantages.

Warren Buffett

If Peter Lynch taught me investing methodologies, Warren Buffett influenced my business understanding and investing philosophy. I read through all of Buffett's partnership and shareholder letters from the 1950s to the present, which completely changed the way I think about business and the philosophy of investing. An investor should forever remember the following three quotes from Buffett.

"It's Far Better to Buy a Wonderful Company at a Fair Price Than a Fair Company at a Wonderful Price"[9]

Lynch placed companies in six categories and taught us what to do with each. Buffett tells us to invest only in the good ones and to buy them at reasonable prices.

Granted, Buffett had tremendous success in his early years by buying marginal businesses on the cheap. But he made most of his money over the long term by investing in wonderful companies at attractive prices. These wonderful companies include the likes of See's Candy and GEICO Insurance. He called GEICO "The Security I Like the Most" more than 60 years ago,[10] and he still calls it that today.

So, there are two questions to answer:

1. What kinds of companies does Warren Buffett consider "wonderful"?
2. What is "fair price"?

Wonderful Companies

These are, according to Buffett, the characteristics of wonderful companies:

1. *A broad and durable competitive advantage, or economic moat*

An economic moat protects a company from its competitors and prevents others from entering its market. It gives the company significant pricing power so that the company can increase its earnings over time.

One indication that a company has a strong economic moat is that it has high profit margins and can maintain, or even grow, its profit margins over the long term. An example, once more, is Moody's. The debt issuers need Moody's more than Moody's needs the debt issuers. They can charge the issuers at their set prices, or the issuers will have to pay even more in the debt market without the ratings. As we described before, even with the help of the governments across the United States and Europe, competitors cannot take away Moody's market share. With this moat, Moody's could maintain high profit margins. Here is the comparison between the operating margins of Moody's and the other two best-run and most profitable companies in the past decade, Apple and Google.

For starters, operating margin is the profit that a business makes before paying interest on its debt and tax. For an example, if a retailer sold $100 of goods that it bought for $60, its gross margin is \$100 – \$60 = \$40. The retailer has to pay business expenses such as rent, salary, and Internet, which costs him \$15. His operating profit will be \$40 – \$15 = \$25. So, the operating margin will be \$25/\$100 = 25%. Operating margin is a good indication of how profitable a business is.

Here are the operating margins (%) of Apple, Google, and Moody's:

Fiscal Year	2006	2007	2008	2009	2010	2011	2012	2013	2014	2015
Apple	13%	18%	19%	27%	28%	31%	35%	29%	29%	30%
Google	33%	31%	30%	35%	35%	31%	25%	23%	25%	26%
Moody's	62%	50%	43%	38%	38%	39%	39%	42%	43%	42%

Moody's, over the past decade, has consistently had much higher operating margins.

2. *Low capex requirement and high returns on invested capital*

An indication of companies that have low capital requirement is that they have high capital turnover and can generate high returns on invested capital. As a result, only a small portion of earnings has to be reinvested in the business.

See's Candy was earning \$4 million a year in 1972. But by 2015 it had earned \$1.9 billion, pretax. Better yet, its growth has required added investment of only \$40 million. Over more than 40 years under the ownership of Berkshire Hathaway, See's needed only \$40 million in capital expenditure and has earned Berkshire \$1.9 billion. This results in a ratio of capex/pretax income of just over 2 percent.

I have calculated the ratio of capex/pretax income of Moody's, Apple, and Google; the result:

Fiscal Year	2006	2007	2008	2009	2010	2011	2012	2013	2014	2015
Apple	23%	20%	17%	10%	11%	22%	17%	18%	18%	16%
Google	47%	42%	40%	10%	37%	28%	24%	51%	63%	50%
Moody's	2%	16%	12%	14%	11%	8%	4%	4%	5%	6%

Clearly, Moody's needs much less capital expenditure for its growth than Apple and Google. The company only needs to buy more furniture and computers for its growth. Capital spending accounted for a mere 6 percent of its net income in 2015; the remaining 94 percent can be used for rewarding shareholders in dividends and share buybacks after paying tax.

Here are the returns on invested capital for these three companies:

Fiscal Year	2006	2007	2008	2009	2010	2011	2012	2013	2014	2015
Apple				192%	92%	70%	59%	38%	35%	40%
Google	76%	53%	46%	54%	62%	57%	44%	37%	34%	33%
Moody's	11,770%		639%	267%	307%	219%	253%	280%	195%	158%

Though both Apple and Google had very high returns on invested capital, Moody's has been higher.

For starters, return on invested capital (ROIC) measures how well a company generates cash flow relative to the capital it has invested in its business. The invested capital is the total of the shareholders' equity and the debt less the cash it has. The higher ROIC is, the more efficient the business is with its capital.

Moody's is better than both Apple and Google in terms of economic moat and capital requirement. But this doesn't guarantee better stock performance, even in the long term, because another factor plays an important role. This constitutes the third characteristic for wonderful companies: growth.

3. *Profitable growth*

This table represents the year-over-year earnings-per-share growth rate (%) of the three companies. The last column is the average growth rate over the past ten years.

Fiscal Year	2006	2007	2008	2009	2010	2011	2012	2013	2014	2015	Average
Apple	45%	73%	37%	69%	67%	83%	60%	–10%	14%	43%	55%
Google	98%	34%	0%	53%	29%	13%	9%	18%	10%	9%	27%
Moody's	40%	0%	–28%	–10%	27%	16%	22%	18%	28%	0%	19%

Both Apple and Google grew much faster than Moody's. The faster growth of these two companies has contributed tremendously to the growth of their intrinsic values, or fair prices. That is the main reason why Apple stock gained almost 1,000 percent over the past decade while Google stock gained about 280 percent and Moody's gained just 80 percent.

Fair Price/Intrinsic Value

Every share of stock represents partial ownership in the company. So, the fair price of the stock is whatever that portion of business is worth, or its "intrinsic value." In principle, the intrinsic value is equal to the discounted value of the cash flow that can be generated by the business during its remaining life, as explained by Buffett.

As history's most successful value investor, Buffett was misunderstood quite often on growth. Many people believed that he didn't care about it, but growth is one of the most important components of his definition of wonderful companies. In his 1951 article, "GEICO: The Security I Like the Most," he determined that GEICO is a growth company.[11] He wrote:

> GEICO qualifies as a legitimate growth company.... In GEICO's case, there is reason to believe that major portion of growth lies ahead.

Of course, he was talking about profitable growth. In his 1992 shareholder letter, he wrote:[12]

> Growth is always a component in the calculation of value, constituting a variable whose importance can range from negligible to enormous and whose impact can be negative as well as positive.

When a company grows profitably and generates positive returns on its invested capital, its intrinsic value grows, too. A wonderful company can grow its value over the long term and reward its shareholders with more earning power over time. In comparison, a marginal business will probably not be able to create value over time. More likely is that it will destroy value. Even if an investor can buy it at a wonderful price, as Buffett did with his textile companies, the results can still be disastrous.

Wouldn't it be better if an investor could buy a wonderful company at a wonderful price? Ideally, yes. But because of the market condition and its size, Buffett changed his requirement on valuation from "a very attractive price" in 1977 to "an attractive price" in 1992, then to "a fair price" in recent years.

I will discuss valuation in depth in Chapter 9.

For most investors who don't have the portfolio-size problems of Buffett, the chance of finding wonderful companies at wonderful prices is far greater. This is one of the many advantages that small investors enjoy.

"It's Crazy to Put Money in Your Twentieth Choice Rather Than Your First Choice"

After all the hard work of finding the wonderful company in which to invest, isn't it obvious that an investor should bet big on it? It's difficult enough to find one good investment idea, let alone 20. Why would an investor put money in his or her twentieth choice instead of his or her first choice?

This quote from Buffett strikes me as obvious, but it is hard to do, and not many investors have the guts to keep a concentrated portfolio. If an investor has confidence in his or her research, he or she won't have difficulty putting as much money as possible in the investment idea, just as Buffett did with GEICO in 1951. After a four-hour meeting with Lorimer Davidson, the then-future CEO at GEICO's headquarters, and learning all he could about GEICO and the insurance industry, Buffett made the stock 75 percent of his $9,800 investment portfolio. "Even so, I felt over-diversified," he wrote.[13] This successful investment would get him off to a great start with his investment career and also jumpstart his net worth. He later wrote:

> Diversification is protection against ignorance. It makes little sense if you know what you are doing.... Wide diversification is only required when investors do not understand what they are doing.
>
> We believe that a policy of portfolio concentration may well decrease risk if it raises, as it should, both the intensity with which an investor thinks about a business and the comfort-level he must feel with its economic characteristics before buying into it.

Therefore, the key to maintaining a concentrated investment portfolio is to understand as much as possible about the business of the company and the industries in which it operates in order to build enough confidence to bet big. With certainty in one's research and compelling long-term convictions, betting big is much easier to do—and guts won't be a requirement.

Buffett continued to write in his 1993 shareholder letter:[14]

> On the other hand, if you are a know-something investor, able to understand business economics and to find five to ten sensibly-priced companies that possess important long-term competitive advantages, conventional diversification makes no sense for you. It is apt simply to hurt your results and increase your risk. I cannot understand why an investor of that sort elects to put money into a business that is his 20th favorite rather than simply adding that money to his top choices—the businesses he understands best and that present the least risk, along with the greatest profit potential. In the words of the prophet Mae West: "Too much of a good thing can be wonderful."

The message is straightforward: Stick to your best ideas. It is improbable for a single person to have unique insights and understanding of dozens of companies across many industries and keep up with the development of these companies over time.

One can argue that investors like Ben Graham, Walter Schloss, and Peter Lynch had a diversified portfolio but still did extremely well. Graham and Schloss invested strictly according to certain key parameters on stock prices and didn't pay much attention to the companies' business and management.[15] Therefore, diversification was needed. Lynch himself owns thousands of stocks. But his advice to part-time stock pickers is to follow 8 to 12 companies because "owning stocks is like having children—don't get involved with more than you can handle."[16] With a concentrated portfolio, Buffett had a much easier life; he can continue to enjoy investing in his eighties and still manages a portfolio that is many times larger than Lynch's.

And, more importantly, betting big is more rewarding. Buffett has run a concentrated portfolio throughout his career, which is a significant reason he had the best track record for so long. To this day, Buffett runs an equity portfolio of more than $128 billion;

70 percent of the portfolio, or almost $90 billion, is concentrated on the top five positions. As of September 30, 2016, these positions are exclusively the wonderful companies at fair prices: Kraft Heinz, Wells Fargo, Coca-Cola, IBM, and American Express.

After finding the handful of wonderful companies at reasonable prices and concentrating investment practices on them, the next thing to do is be patient, which brings up the third key point I learned from Buffett:

"Our Favorite Holding Period Is Forever"

One common mistake investors make is to sell the winners for a quick profit and hang onto the ones that did poorly. Lynch calls such behavior cutting the flowers and watering the weeds. It is hard to find the wonderful companies at reasonable prices, so now it is time to hang onto them as long as the fundamentals hold and the valuation is reasonable. This is the complete Buffett quote, from his 1998 shareholder letter, about holding time:[17]

> In fact, when we own portions of outstanding businesses with outstanding managements, our favorite holding period is forever.

During the holding time, two things happen.

1. The gap between the intrinsic value and the price paid closes over time.
2. The intrinsic value of the business grows over time.

Over the long term, the contribution from the growth of the value can be so high that the price would no longer be that critical. Consider Buffett's purchase of See's Candy in 1972: The family controlling See's wanted $30 million, but Buffett didn't want to pay more than $25 million. Luckily, the sellers took his $25 million bid, or Berkshire would have missed out on the $1.9 billion in earnings for the $5 million difference.[18]

Buying a stock with the intention of holding for a long time also works conversely. If you think long term during your research, the noise that pervades will no longer matter. You can focus on the things that matter over the long term, such as the quality of the business, the industry in which it operates, and its intrinsic value.

Donald Yacktman

Peter Lynch could find good ideas in all six of his categories; Warren Buffett tells us to invest in the good ones among them. Donald Yacktman goes a step further and says that we should simply invest in the good companies that are not cyclical.

Yacktman is probably not as well-known as Lynch and Buffett. He is the founder of the firm that bears his name, Yacktman Asset Management, which manages more than $17 billion as of 2016. Yacktman built his reputation in the 1980s by producing outstanding results as a fund manager at American Shares Fund. He started his own fund in 1992, and the fund's assets grew to $1.1 billion by 1997. The tech bubble was then speeding up, but Yacktman was still investing in the old-fashioned way of buying undervalued profitable companies. His fund was lagging in the market so much that investors started to quickly pull their money. In 1998, some of the fund's directors wanted him to go, and only a fierce proxy fight kept Donald Yacktman at Yacktman Asset Management. By 2000, the fund's assets shrank to a mere $70 million, and finally his strategy of value investing started to work again. In 2000, Yacktman's fund outperformed the S&P 500 by 20 percent; in 2001, by 31 percent; and in 2002, by 33 percent. His fund continued to do extremely well during the financial bubble in 2008 and 2009, beating the S&P 500 by 11 percent during the market crash in 2008 and 33 percent during the market recovery in 2009. I extend my sympathy to those shareholders who withdrew from the fund and put their money into high-flying technology funds.

The core investing philosophy of Yacktman is viewing stocks as bonds, which means thinking in terms of the rate of return from the stock, just like with bonds. The key points of his strategy are related to the business type, the management, and the investment hurdle.

Buy Good Businesses That Are Not Cyclical

Like Buffett, Yacktman tells investors to commit only to good businesses. But he goes into more detail and says to invest only in good businesses that are not cyclical and to invest only in companies whose products have a short customer repurchase cycle and long product cycles. Good examples of such products are mostly consumer staples such as toothpaste, baking soda, and condoms. The products are consumed daily by customers and will need to be purchased again quickly, no matter how the economy is doing. Also, consumers usually purchase them with cash instead of credit. These companies don't have to continually invent new technologies and keep competing with new generations of products. Coca-Cola has been selling the same drink for many decades, which represents the long product cycle.

Such companies are clearly evidenced in his portfolio in the Yacktman Fund, as his largest holdings at the time of this writing are Procter & Gamble, PepsiCo, and Coca-Cola. Coca-Cola is also one of Buffett's largest holdings.

And like Buffett, Yacktman prefers companies with a low capital requirement for growth. This kind of company can generate cash while growing, and due to low capital investment, there is no need for borrowing, and the overall business risk is much lower.

Therefore, an investor should avoid companies that have long customer repurchase cycles, such as automakers. These businesses are highly cyclical and immensely competitive, and customers tend to buy cars only when the economy is good. The companies must develop new car models to stay competitive, and they also need to invest in their manufacturing facility to keep abreast of the latest technology, which requires large capital investments for growth.

Consider my former employer, a telecom equipment maker. Its products are a lot like cars: Customers only buy when the economy is good; and it takes a tremendous amount of capital and at least five years to develop a new generation of product, but the product rarely lasts more than a generation before it is obsolete. Bad business! I'm glad to be out of there.

Management

The capability of management is a key factor for the long-term success of a company, especially for the business that requires more than an idiot to run. Buffett has written many times that he looks for "honest and capable management" in the companies he buys, but hedge fund manager Mohnish Pabrai once said that all CEOs are good salespeople. It is hard to know if they are capable just from listening to how they talk.

Yacktman looks at what the management does and does not do with the cash the company generates. A shareholder-oriented management team will do the following, as Yacktman described during his keynote address at the 2016 GuruFocus Value Conference: The management will *not* overcompensate themselves; they will spend the cash earned by the company in these areas and in this order:

1. *Reinvest:* They will reinvest cash back into the business for growth.
2. *Acquisitions:* If they still have more cash than needed, they will grow the business by making acquisitions. An investor needs to be careful here, looking at their past track record with acquisitions. Most of the big acquisitions don't work out as expected.
3. *Buyback:* They buy back stocks if they still have more money than they can spend. The investor wants to make sure he or she doesn't pay too much buying back their own stocks, which destroys value for the remaining shareholders.
4. They reduce debt.
5. They pay more dividends.

Buffett also described in detail how management should spend excess cash in his 2012 shareholder letter.[19] His thinking is in line with what Yacktman believes.

Therefore, in judging the quality of the management, the investor should watch carefully how they allocate capital and disregard how they talk. For businesses like those that could be run by an idiot, the skills of the management have a lesser impact on the business. Take McDonald's, as I referenced earlier. The company went through many CEOs during the past decade and had some hiccups, but it still does very well. However, for the businesses that have more complex products and operations, the management capability can make a huge impact on results.

Set Your Hurdle Rate

A key factor of Yacktman's long-term success is that he set a hurdle rate to act on. He didn't buy tech stocks during the tech bubble because the potential rate of return didn't make sense. His cash positions were higher than normal before the burst of the financial bubble in 2006 because not many stocks can hit his hurdle rate. As the financial bubble burst in 2008 and 2009, many of the stocks he had wanted to buy for a long time were positioned to generate much higher returns than his hurdle rate, so he poured all his cash into stocks. With this discipline regarding his hurdle rate, he outperformed the market in both ways during the market crash in 2008 and the market recovery in 2009. In 2008, when the S&P 500 lost 37 percent, his fund did better by 11 percent because he held more cash. In 2009, when the S&P 500 gained 26.5 percent, his fund gained 60 percent because he bought into beaten-down stocks with the cash that had stayed on hand.

The hurdle rate is based on valuation or dividend yield or the expected return for the stocks. In Yacktman's case, he uses a term called "forward rate of return," which is the annual average return that the stock is expected to generate in the next seven to ten years. I will detail the calculation and application of Yacktman's "forward rate of return" in Chapter 9.

The hurdle rate works for investors in both directions of the market. When the market is going up, the hurdle rate will protect investors from buying overvalued stocks. When the market is going down, those who stick to the hurdle rate will know when to pull the trigger.

Have I made it sound too easy? It certainly is not easy. When the stock market keeps going up, no stocks meet your hurdle rate and you remain on the sidelines. But the market continues its uptrend. It is extremely hard to watch your portfolios underperform and miss all the gains, and this can go on for years and years; this is especially true for the professional investors, as their performances are watched monthly, if not daily. Those who stick to their hurdle rates will see themselves underperforming when the market valuation is high and continues to go higher. Look no further than Yacktman. After delivering great performances from 2007 through 2011, his fund is again underperforming. He just holds too much cash to match the performance of the S&P 500, which is always fully invested. At this time, even Buffett is underperforming.

It is not easy to stick to your hurdle rate during the downward market, either. Finally, the market is going down and many of the stocks you always wanted to buy have hit your hurdle rate. But it is scary because the market is crashing. The stock market always goes down faster than it goes up. It takes much longer to blow a bubble than to burst it. The stock you want to buy is going down quickly; if you buy it now, you will soon find that you have lost 10 percent, 20 percent, or even more in a few short days. But if you don't buy and wait for a better price, you may find that you have missed the opportunity—again.

Therefore, setting a hurdle rate and sticking to it is very hard to do, but it is extremely important for the long-term success of investors. Only those who are willing to, and have the luxury of being able to, sacrifice short-term performance can outperform in the long term.

What to do when no stock meets your hurdle rate? This is a good time to do research. It is a good time to build a watch list for the wonderful-business companies you would buy at a lower price so that you are ready when the time comes.

■ ■ ■

Although I summarized what I learned from Peter Lynch, Warren Buffett, and Donald Yacktman in three distinct areas, all three have touched on all areas. Many other investors have inspired me through their writings, too; I have also been reading the letters of Howard Marks of Oaktree Capital, Jeremy Grantham of GMO, Bill Nygren of Oakmark Funds, Robert Rodriguez of FPA Capital, and Steven Romick of FPA Crescent Fund. The list goes on and on.

I have learned tremendously. As I have mentioned, investing *can* be learned.

Buffett, the genius and the most successful investor of all time, has covered every topic related to business and investing in his letters to Berkshire Hathaway shareholders. These topics range from the economy to business operations such as corporate governance, management qualities, accounting, tax, and mergers and acquisitions. He offers insight into the businesses of insurance, banking, retail, airlines, newspapers, and utilities—and of course, investing. His shareholder letters should be recommended reading for all students in business schools and for anyone who is serious about business management and investing. If you haven't done so, I highly recommend you get started reading immediately after you finish this book.

My learning changed me, and I now look at everything in life, even if it is not related to business and investing, from a totally different angle. Of course, I apply what I learned in my own practice of investing research, and in the following chapters I will detail how to apply this knowledge in your investing. I hope to establish the right investing framework so that you can invest in one with a solid foundation and avoid many of the mistakes that investors could have averted, and ultimately achieve long-term success.

As I was reading and rereading Buffett's shareholder letters, I was consistently amazed at how much Buffett knows about business and investing. Buffett has said many times that he "was wired at birth to allocate capital," and that the value investing concept of "buying dollar bills for 40 cents takes immediately to people."[20] But, even if the value investing concept takes you immediately, you still need to know how to find that dollar bill selling for 40 cents. Perhaps Buffett was wired at birth to be a great investor, but the knowledge certainly didn't come at birth. He learned from his father, Howard Buffett, and from Benjamin Graham, Philip Fisher, Charlie Munger, and many others, and from the many books and reports he's read. He is "one of the best learning machines on this earth," as his long-term partner Charlie Munger puts it. Munger continued:

> Warren was lucky that he could still learn effectively and build his skills, even after he reached retirement age. Warren's investing skills have markedly increased since he turned 65.[21]

When he was once asked how one could get to know so much, Buffett pointed to a stack of books and reports and said, "Read five hundred pages like this every day. That's how knowledge builds up, like compound interest."[22] It is now reported that Todd Combs, one of Buffett's successors, is reading up to 1,000 pages a day![23]

I want to finish this chapter with a quote from Munger that echoes the one at the beginning:

> I constantly see people rise in life who are not the smartest, sometimes not even the most diligent, but they are learning machines. They go to bed every night a little wiser than they were when they got up and boy does that help, particularly when you have a long run ahead of you.[24]

CHAPTER 2

Deep-Value Investing and Its Inherent Problems

"Don't let the tall weeds cast a shadow on the beautiful flowers in your garden."

—Steve Maraboli[1]

After the bursting of the tech bubble, many of the once high-flying tech stocks were sold off without regard to the price. By October 2002, the stock of Oplink, the fiber optics company I'd bought, dropped from its two-year-prior price of $250 to $4.5 a share (split adjusted). Concurrently, the company had the net cash per share of over $8, which means that if the company had ceased its operations, eliminated all its other assets, and distributed the cash to its shareholders, these shareholders would have almost immediately doubled their money. Therefore, at some point, even an originally poor investment can become a pretty good one if the price is right.

This is an example of deep-value investing, a strategy that focuses on buying the stocks of the company at a deep discount against the value of its assets. The approach was theorized by the founding father of value investing and the mentor of Warren Buffett, Benjamin Graham.[2]

Deep-Value Investing

The idea of deep-value investing is straightforward; it is simply "buying dollar bills for 40 cents," as explained by Buffett, who in his early years experienced tremendous success practicing deep-value investing.[3] Deep-value investors try to buy the stock of a company for a price that is discounted from the assessed value of the assets, then wait for the gap between the price and the value to close. Deep-value investors require a minimum gap between the price and the assessed value in order to buy. This minimum gap is called the margin of safety, which is important to protect investors from errors occurring during the assessment of the value.

The idea is illustrated in Figure 2.1.

Over time, the gap between the price and the value may shrink, and deep-value investors can profit from selling the stock at a higher price, which might be closer to the value of the stock.

Benjamin Graham and Walter Schloss were deep-value investors.[4] Graham said in his classic book, *The Intelligent Investor,* that to avoid errors and ignorance, it is safer to have a diversified portfolio, which may consist of more than a hundred companies.[5] In assessing what the stock is worth, or its value, deep-value investors focus on the balance sheet of the company and have no interest in its operations. There are four ways to estimate the company's value, depending on how conservatively investors want to go with the valuation.

Tangible Book Value

In this approach, the company is only worth the value of its tangible assets, such as cash, receivables, inventories, buildings, and equipment after paying all the debt and other liabilities. Its intangible assets, such as goodwill, patents, trademarks, brands, and business

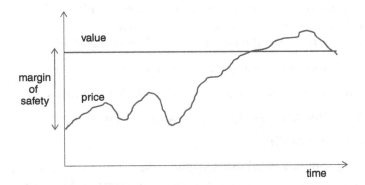

Figure 2.1   Value Investing and Margin of Safety

operations are considered worth nothing. Therefore, the value of per share is calculated as:

Tangible book per share

=(Total assets–Total liabilities–Preferred stock–Intangible assets)/

Shares outstanding

This approach is seemingly a conservative way of estimating a company's value, but the investor can go even more conservatively.

Net Current Asset Value

To be more conservative and careful in the valuation, we assign no value to the business's long-term assets such as buildings, land, and equipment. Only its current assets are taken into account for the calculation because all the liabilities are actual and must be paid, so the net current asset value (NCAV) of a company is calculated as:

NCAV per share

= (Current assets – Total liabilities – Preferred stock)/

Shares outstanding

Risk still exists with this approach because not every current asset is worth its listed value. An even more conservative evaluation is the net-net working capital.

Net-Net Working Capital

In this approach, the inventory and the receivables are discounted to their book value and any prepaid expenses are considered worth nothing, but the liabilities are still real. It is defined as:

Net-Net Working Capital (NNWC) per share

= (Cash and short-term investments + (0.75 * accounts receivable)

+ (0.5 * inventory) – Total liabilities – Preferred stock)/

Shares outstanding

In the net-net working capital valuation, cash is counted as 100 percent, accounts receivable as 75 percent of book value, and inventories as 50 percent of their value. Everything else is worth nothing and the liabilities are paid in full. This is assuming that in a fire-sale the value of the company is what is left for shareholders.

Net Cash

In the net cash valuation, only the cash and short-term investments of the company are used for the calculation. Everything else is considered worth nothing:

Net-cash per share

= (Cash and short-term investments − Total liabilities

− Preferred stock)/Shares outstanding

It seems inconceivable that anyone would sell a portion of a company at a price that is far below its liquidation value, but this does happen, especially during market panics. Even as of July 2016, the stock market has reached an all-time high, yet some stocks are still sold at a price far below their liquidation value. In the table below, I list some of them. All numbers are per-share numbers for July 19, 2016.

	Tangible Book Value	NCAV	Net-Net Working Capital	Net-Cash	Price
Emerson Radio Corp.	$ 1.99	$ 1.93	$ 1.75	$ 1.75	$ 0.68
Adverum Biotechnologies Inc.	$ 8.92	$ 8.78	$ 8.73	$ 8.70	$ 3.07
Carbylan Therapeutics Inc.	$ 1.64	$ 1.63	$ 1.59	$ 1.59	$ 0.59

The numbers are decreasing from tangible book to NCAV to net-net working capital to net cash, as they are more conservative in calculation in that order.

These numbers are taken from GuruFocus.com, where you can find all these numbers, for every stock, as both current and historical values. You can also screen stocks that are sold below their liquidation values with GuruFocus's All-In-One Screener[6] and Ben Graham's Net-Net Screener.[7]

It seems obvious that investors are not in a position to lose money if they buy stocks at far below their liquidation values, which is what Graham did. He wrote in *The Intelligent Investor*.[8]

It always seemed, and still seems, ridiculously simple to say that if one can acquire a diversified group of stocks at a price less than the applicable net current assets alone ... the results should be quite satisfactory.

He continued:

The idea here was to acquire as many issues as possible at a cost for each of less than their book value in terms of net-current-assets alone—i.e., giving no value to the plant account and other assets. Our purchases were made typically at two-thirds or less of such stripped-down asset value. In most years we carried a wide diversification here—at least 100 different issues.

Graham looked for companies whose market values were less than two-thirds of their net-current-asset values. GuruFocus has created the Graham Bargain Screener to screen for these net-current-asset bargains, which can also be found at: http://www.gurufocus.com/grahamncav.php.

The risk in investing in these companies is that most of them are not well-run and may be continuously losing money. To reduce the risk, GuruFocus added the option that users can filter for companies that have positive operating cash flow. In this way, the companies will likely be able to maintain their operations without burning through their cash.

According to Graham, some of these companies may well become insolvent as economic conditions worsen, so it is important to hold a diversified basket of them.

Though the strategy worked well for Graham, these bargains are no longer around for modern value investors seeking to build a diversified portfolio. During the drastic decline of the stock market in 2008, this screener had a long list, but it has gradually dwindled.

My experience with Ben Graham Net Current Asset Bargains has been mixed. Just as Graham described, when you can locate many of them, the strategy works well. But if you cannot, the ones you do find will likely not bring success.

For instance, following are the top-20 stocks generated by the screener on December 26, 2008. S&P 500 was 872 and had lost more than 40 percent from its peak in 2007. It is, as of this writing, 2163. The performances of the 20 stocks through July 2011 are displayed here:

December 2008 Net-Net Working Capital Portfolio (S&P 500 = 872)

Symbol	Price on Dec. 26, 2008	Prices as of July 13, 2011	Change %	Comment
Heelys Inc.	2.52	2.24	–11%	
Valpey Fisher Corp.	1.45	2.7	86%	
Solta Medical, Inc.	1.35	2.6	93%	
Emerson Radio Corp.	0.51	1.97	286%	
Orbotech Ltd.	4.06	12.35	204%	
Silicon Graphics International Corp.	3.76	15.87	322%	
NUCRYST Pharmaceuticals Corporation	0.85	1.77	108%	Acquired
PECO II Inc.	2.1	5.86	179%	Acquired
Dataram Corp.	1.15	1.59	38%	
Mattson Technology Inc.	1.2	1.94	62%	
ACS Motion Control Ltd.	0.91	1.4	54%	
Avanex Corp.	1.04	3.256	213%	Acquired
LinkTone	1.13	0.9701	–14%	
PDI Inc.	3.39	7.72	128%	
Actions Semiconductor Co. Ltd.	1.6	2.15	34%	
Soapstone Networks Inc.	2.46	0.01	–100%	
Transcept Pharmaceuticals Inc.	5.45	8.59	58%	
ValueVision Media Inc.	0.29	8.29	2759%	
Allianz SE	10.14	12.82	26%	
GSI Group Inc.	1.65	11.99	627%	
		Average	**257.6%**	

Among these stocks, a complete loss occurred with only one company, Soapstone Networks Inc. Three companies were acquired at premiums and gains were all more than 100 percent. As a group, these 20 stocks have averaged a gain of 257 percent. By comparison, for the same period, the S&P 500 gained 48.5 percent and the

Nasdaq index gained 82 percent. Seventeen of the 20 stocks had positive returns, the greatest being ValueVision Media Inc., which gained more than 2,700 percent over a period of two-and-a-half years. GSI Group Inc. gained more than 600 percent; Silicon Graphics International Corp. gained more than 300 percent; Emerson Radio Corp. gained more than 280 percent. (All numbers exclude dividends.) The net-current-asset value bargains did extremely well, especially during the 12 months when the gain was more than 150 percent.

As the market ticked higher, the number of these bargains decreased. By October 2009, the S&P 500 recovered some of the losses caused by the financial crisis in 2008 and moved back above 1000; we found 12 of these bargains, which are reflected here:

October 2009 Net-Net Working Capital Portfolio
(S&P 500 = 1020)

Company	Price($)
The9 Ltd.	7.57
Orsus Xelent Technologies Inc.	9.36
Heelys Inc.	2.15
eLong Inc.	9.74
TSR Inc.	4.1
Netlist Inc.	0.69
Forward Industries Inc.	1.72
United American Healthcare Corp.	0.99
Optibase Ltd.	6.35
magicJack VocalTec Ltd.	4.88
American Learning Corp.	0.52
MGT Capital Investments Inc.	15

Following are the performances of the portfolio over the next four years:

Year	Bargain Portfolio	SP 500	Nasdaq
Oct. 2009–Sept. 2010	50.00%	9.75%	13.38%
Oct. 2010–Sept. 2011	−17.00%	−1.29%	1.88%
Oct. 2011–Sept. 2012	−2.00%	24.68%	25.69%
Oct. 2012–Sept. 2013	−28.00%	17.43%	24.23%

In the first year, this bargain portfolio delivered a very strong performance and investors would have benefited tremendously from selling it after 12 months, but if the holding time grew longer, the gain would have gradually diminished.

However, as we continued to watch the performance of these net-current-asset bargains, the portfolios we generated after 2011 did not perform well. As a group, they often underperformed the S&P 500 by significant margins.

Listed here is an NCAV bargain portfolio generated in April 2011, when the S&P 500 was above 1300.

April 2011 Net-Net Working Capital Portfolio (S&P 500 = 1332)

Company	Price($)
China TechFaith Wireless Comm Tech Ltd.	21.6
Blucora Inc.	8.79
China-biotics Inc.	8.38
Jiangbo Pharmaceuticals Inc.	4.43
Noah Education Holdings Ltd.	2.16
eLong Inc.	14.25
Gencor Industries Inc.	7.85
Vicon Industries Inc.	4.75
TSR Inc.	4.99
Maxygen Inc.	5.21
Comarco Inc.	0.31
Actions Semiconductor Co Ltd.	2.44
Meade Instruments Corp.	3.66
BroadVision Inc.	14.45
Qualstar Corp.	10.74
Merus Labs International Inc.	1.62
Peerless Systems Corp.	3.16
Cytokinetics Inc.	9.06

Reflected here is the performance of April 2011's NCAV bargain portfolio during the 12-month periods afterward:

Bargain Portfolio April 2011	Bargain Portfolio	S&P 500	Nasdaq
April 2011–March 2012	–10%	7.21%	12.70%
April 2012–March 2013	–20%	11.41%	5.69%
April 2013–March 2014	11%	18.38%	27.18
April 2014–March 2015	–30%	10.51%	18.5

This net-assets-bargain portfolio underperformed the indices from the very beginning and would continue to generate deep losses in all the periods following, even as the broad market continued to gain.

As we continued to observe the performance of deep-bargain portfolios, we initially didn't have many to include in the portfolio with enough margin of safety. If we invested in the ones that appeared, the performance was typically poor and significantly lagged the market.

Compared with Graham's time, finding companies that have large displaced prices relative to their liquidation values is much easier due to the advances of technology. As a result, the market is getting crowded and not many deep bargains exist. Especially true in recent years, when the interest rate has been low, the valuations for all assets have been lifted to much higher levels, and it therefore becomes difficult to find deep bargains relative to the net assets on a company's balance sheet.

The best time to invest in these deep bargains is when you can find plenty of them, especially when panic and forced selling are prevalent in the market due to a market crash. During such a period, many stocks that deserve higher valuations are also beaten down on prices, especially those with relatively poor business fundamentals. When the overall market valuation is high and everything else is rising, those dropping and appearing in the deep-bargain screener probably deserved to be traded by low valuations. Their stock prices were likely low for the right reasons, and buying these would likely have resulted in steep losses, as I observed in the years after 2011. Therefore, when it comes to deep-value investing, investors need to be cautious and aware of this approach's inherent problems.

The Problem with Deep-Value Investing

Buffett coined the term "cigar-butt investing" for the strategy of buying mediocre businesses at prices that are much lower than the companies' net-asset values. He said the approach is like "a cigar butt found on the street that has only one puff left in it [and] may not offer much of a smoke, but the 'bargain purchase' will make that puff all profit."[9]

There are several problems with this approach:

Erosion of Value Over Time

Mediocre businesses do not create value for their shareholders; instead, they destroy business value over time. So, the relationship between value and price is not what it looks like in Figure 2.1 and is closer to what is represented in Figure 2.2.

Therefore, the value of the business can decline and the initial margin of safety may gradually shrink, even if the stock price doesn't go up. Investors need to be lucky enough to have the stock prices rise in time and sell before prices drop again following the intrinsic value of the business.

Just as Buffett wrote in his 1989 shareholder letter: "Time is the friend of the wonderful business, the enemy of the mediocre."[10]

Because he paid dear prices for buying unpromising businesses, Buffett learned his lessons. He considered his buying of the control of Berkshire Hathaway his biggest mistake, which eventually cost Buffett and his partners $100 billion.[11] The stock was sold at a discount to its net-net working capital and less than half of its book value, but because of Berkshire Hathaway's operating loss and share repurchasing of stocks, its net worth had fallen from $55 million in 1964 to $22 million in 1967. At the time, Buffett also bought a well-managed retailer at a substantial discount from book value, but three years later he "was lucky" to sell it at the same price.[12]

This can also be seen from the October 2009 net-net working capital bargain portfolio shown above. In the first 12 months, the

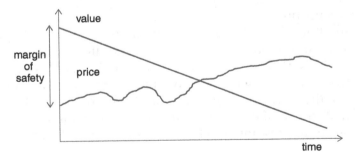

Figure 2.2   Price vs. Value for Mediocre Business

portfolio had substantially higher returns than the market. But in the three years that followed, it gave up all its gains while the stock market continued to march higher.

Timing and Pain

Buy these bargain portfolios when you can find plenty of them, but if the broad market is in quick decline, like in 2008, the bargain portfolio will be very likely to lose much more than the general market. If the decline lasts longer, many of the companies in the portfolio may suffer steeper operating losses and may even go out of business. It is much more painful to hold such a portfolio in bad times, as anyone who owns these stocks during bear markets or recessions will attest—and lose much sleep over!

In addition, because of the quick erosion of business value, selling the deep-asset bargains quickly is key, even if stock prices do not appreciate. The biggest profits are usually achieved within the first 12 months. That is why Charlie Munger said, "If you buy something because it's undervalued, then you have to think about selling it when it approaches your calculation of its intrinsic value. That's hard."[13]

Buffett likens buying mediocre businesses at deep bargain prices for a quick profit to dating without the intent of getting married. In that situation, it is essential to end the courtship at the right time and before the relationship turns sour.

Not Enough Stocks Qualify

To avoid errors and disasters caused by single stocks in the deep-bargain portfolio, it is important to have a diversified group of them. But when the market valuation is high, it is just not possible to find enough stocks to satisfy the diversification requirement. This is the situation that emerged in 2012. GuruFocus's Net-Current-Asset-Bargain is only able to generate a handful of stocks in the U.S. market; they simply dried up as the market continued to tick higher. This situation may last a long time, as the close-to-zero interest rate has lifted the valuations of all assets.

Tax Inefficiency

Because of the short holding time, any gain from the portfolio is subject to the same tax rate as the investor's income tax for U.S.

investors, unless it is in a retirement account. For those in the highest tax bracket, close to 40 percent of gains will have to be paid every year. This drastically reduces the overall return over the long term.

■ ■ ■

Though buying deep-asset bargains can be very profitable, this strategy comes with a much higher mental cost to investors. More importantly, business deterioration and the erosion of value put investors in a riskier position. As a result, they need to strictly follow the rules of maintaining a diversified portfolio and selling within 12 months whether investments worked out or not.

The approach should be to focus on small companies with liquid balance sheets. If a lot of hard assets such as equipment and buildings are involved, the liquidation process can be long and costly, which may eat up all the value the assets have. Buffett had first-hand experience with this. When Berkshire Hathaway finally shut down its textile business and was liquidating, the equipment that originally cost $13 million was still in usable condition and had a current book value of $866,000. The gross proceed from the sale of the equipment was $163,122. After the pre- and post-sale costs, the net proceed was less than zero.[14]

It is very dangerous and costly to hold onto the companies that have complex businesses and illiquid assets. You will get stuck with them while hoping the business will turn around, just as Buffett did with the original textile business of Berkshire Hathaway. If buying mediocre businesses at deep bargain prices for a quick profit is like a date without the intent of getting married, buying them and getting involved long term is like a marriage without love. A lot of other things need to be right to work things out, and it will never be a happy marriage.

One such case, ongoing for the past several years, involves Bruce Berkowitz of Fairholme Fund, one of the best-performing mutual fund managers in the first decade of this century. It has cost both him and his shareholders dearly.

Berkowitz has owned a large position in Sears Holdings, the struggling retailer, for more than a decade. The stock was trading at above $160 before spinoffs, and although he was well aware of the problems with the company's deteriorating retail business, he has long believed that Sears has tremendous values in its real-estate portfolio and its businesses, and these values can be realized by selling the businesses and real estate. By February 2014, the stock had lost more than 70 percent and was traded at $38, and Berkowitz believed that Sears' net assets exceeded $150 in value. He wrote in February 2014: "If our research is accurate, Sears' market price of $38 [is expected] to increase to this value over time."[15] Two-and-a-half years later, the stock is traded at below $10. Even if we added back the value from the spinoff of Lands' End and the right to buy Seritage at a discount, the stock has lost more than another 70 percent. Berkowitz is continuing to buy more Sears.

In the meantime, Sears has been doing everything to unlock value under the leadership of another supposedly capable value investor and financier, Eddie Lampert. Sears spun off Orchard Supply Hardware in January 2012 at above $20 and it now trades at 20 cents. The company couldn't compete with Home Depot and Lowe's, whether it was on its own or under Sears, and is now bankrupt. Another spinoff, Sears Canada, was never profitable after the spinoff at $18.5 a share in October 2012; the stock has since lost more than 80 percent and is on its own way to bankruptcy. The Seritage spinoff has been doing relatively well so far, but what the original shareholders received was the right to buy shares at $29.5 instead of simply getting the shares outright as with other spinoffs. Sears itself has been losing money every year for the past five. Most of the $2.7 billion proceeds from selling its primary properties to Seritage was used to cover the cash drain from its operating loss in 2015 alone. What value does it really unlock?

Sears also bought back a lot of shares over the years to "return" capital to shareholders. But for a company that kept losing money, the remaining shareholders only saw their share of loss get bigger and their share of business value drained faster.

One may argue that Sears shareholders could have sold the shares of Orchard Supply and Sears Canada after the spinoffs and benefited by doing so. I would argue that Sears shareholders should have long ago sold their shares altogether. The same is true for Berkowitz. His Fairholme shareholders would have been much better served ten years ago if he had sold Sears at above $160, or six years ago at above $70, or four years ago at above $40, or two years ago at above $30. The stock is now traded at below $10 and he is still not giving up. Instead, he is buying more because the stock is even more "undervalued." The cost to Fairholme shareholders has been steep. The fund underperformed the S&P 500 by a total of more than 35 percent in the last three years and more than 50 percent in the last five years. Should I also talk about the lost opportunities?

The drama continues. Sears is spending heavily trying to turn around its beleaguered money-losing retail business and is hoping to compete against the likes of Amazon and Wal-Mart. Berkowitz has now joined the board of Sears. Such a move will definitely add more to his mental and psychological cost. The surprises just kept coming. Sears' pension fund burned $2 billion in the last several years, which as of today is more than double of the entire market cap of the company. The unlocking of value took longer than expected, which means more value is about to be eroded. In May 2016, Berkowitz thought that the problem with the pension obligation should improve, as the Fed's interest rate hike seemed imminent,[16] only to see the interest rate continue to drop. Now he is expecting the retail losses to stop in 2016, which is unlikely as the company's loss keeps getting bigger each quarter. In the meantime, the company burned through another $700 million in the first quarter of 2016 and issued about the same amount of debt to maintain its cash balance.

Doesn't this sound like a hole that keeps getting deeper? Why would I, as an investor, want to get involved in this mess and witness things deteriorating, hoping the situation will improve? Even if it works out eventually, which to me is very unlikely, the mental and psychological drain is simply not worth it.

Buffett said it best:[17]

> Unless you are a liquidator, that kind of approach to buying businesses is foolish. First, the original 'bargain' price probably will not turn out to be such a steal after all. In a difficult business, no sooner is one problem solved than another surfaces—never is there just one cockroach in the kitchen. Second, any initial advantage you secure will be quickly eroded by the low return that the business earns ...

There are better ways to make money.

CHAPTER 3

Buy Only Good Companies!

"Take a simple idea and take it seriously."

—Charlie Munger

Yes, there are better ways to make money!

Instead of buying companies with deteriorating values on the cheap and hoping things will improve, why not buy companies that grow value over time? Warren Buffett summarized in a single sentence the priceless lessons he learned from his personal "bargain-purchase folly." These words should forever remain in the minds of investors: "It's far better to buy a wonderful company at a fair price than a fair company at a wonderful price."

This is the philosophy that Donald Yacktman has relied on to help him build one of the best long-term track records. In the early 1990s, one of his sons suggested that he buy Chrysler. The stock was traded at around $10 and seemed like a bargain, but he told his son: "I think you are going to make money, but I just don't want to be in there. I just don't like the business."

Yacktman explained his reasoning in his keynote address at the 2016 GuruFocus Value Conference:

> To me it is like going into a factory where you have all these assets in there, but they are not functioning. What a steal if I am paying twenty cents on a dollar; but, on the other hand, if I go into another factory and it is just humming .... To me the value is in the cash flow, not in the assets. It is the cash generated by the assets where the real value is coming in.

Appreciate the point, Sears shareholders? Though the company has assets that seem valuable, when was the last time you actually shopped at Sears?

Yacktman likens buying companies that have mediocre business at bargain prices to riding moving sidewalks, and buying good companies to riding escalators—it is an escalator that keeps raising the value of the business. So, as investors, we should focus on these value escalators and *buy only good companies!*

Even if deep bargains exist among marginal businesses, investors should ignore these and instead pay attention to good companies. Good companies are what we want to buy, even if they don't look like a steal.

So, what kind of company is considered a good company?

What Are Good Companies?

A good company is one that can continuously grow value through its operations. It will be worth more tomorrow than it is today. As opposed to mediocre businesses that erode value over time, a good business can grow its value and do so consistently, as in Yacktman's analogy. The value of the company rises higher and higher and time is its friend.

The relationship between the value and price of good companies is illustrated in Figure 3.1. The value of the business is growing; over time, the stock price will follow the value and also move higher.

Because the value of the business is growing—much like love in a marriage—many problems cease to exist. I hope you like this story:

A marriage counselor was giving a seminar to a room filled with people seeking marital advice. He projected his first slide, the key to a successful marriage, which showed just one phrase: "Love each other, forever." Participants started to shake their heads and said the sentiment was hard to put into practice. Then the marriage counselor put up his second slide, which said: "If you cannot do that, now you need to follow these four rules: (1) Compromise, tolerate, and forgive. (2) Make it a habit to compromise, tolerate, and forgive. (3) Pretend to be a fool. (4) Make that a habit, too." The participants grew more vocal, saying these four rules are impossible to follow. Waiting until they quieted down, the counselor put up his third slide, which said: "If you cannot follow these four rules, now you

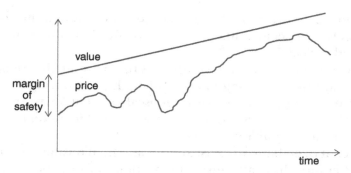

Figure 3.1   Price vs. Value for Good Businesses

need to do these 16 things right: (1) Don't lose your tempers at the same time. (2) Don't yell unless it is an emergency. (3) When getting into an argument, let your spouse win. (4) Don't let an argument last overnight. (5) Always be ready to apologize..." After reading these, some laughed and some sighed. The counselor then showed his fourth slide, which said: "If you still cannot follow 16 rules, now you need to do these 256 things right..."

So, life is much easier if you can find companies that are growing their value. The following offer some of the advantages of buying good companies:

No Worries About Timing

Unlike buying mediocre businesses, where investors are forced to sell if the price is getting close to the value and they need to sell before the value erosion hurts the stock price, you only need to buy the stock at a reasonable price, and you don't have to worry about selling. You can indeed hold the stock forever because its value keeps going up. Of course, stock prices fluctuate, but they always follow the direction of value over the course of time.

More Forgiving with Purchase Price

A good company deserves a higher valuation. It is possible that you paid a slightly higher price than you wanted to pay for the stock, which lowers your overall rate of return, but time is on your side and your long holding time minimizes the impact of the higher purchase price to your overall return. Also, you will always find the opportunity to add to your position at lower valuations, though not necessarily at lower prices.

Buffett was reluctant to pay $25 million for See's Candy in 1972. Later he felt lucky that the seller accepted the price and it was such a bargain, although it didn't seem to be one to him at the time. Missing the opportunity to buy good companies at reasonable prices can cost much more!

No Risk of Permanent Loss of Capital

As Peter Lynch said, "Companies that have no debt can't go bankrupt." Good companies have a strong balance sheet and can consistently generate profit. Their value continues to accumulate. Investors will sooner or later profit from holding good companies. In addition, an investor with the sense of buying good companies is also unlikely to pay an outrageous price for a stock. Again, time is on your side.

More Tax-Efficient

Clearly, with a long holding time, investors can grow their capital and defer tax payments on the capital gain, as long as they don't sell. Even if the investor does sell, the gain is taxed at a lower tax rate. Berkshire Hathaway has owned Coca-Cola for three decades and has $16 billion of capital gain on it, but Buffett hasn't paid a penny of capital gain tax because he hasn't sold any Coca-Cola shares.

You Sleep Better

You don't have to stay alert with a business that is steadily growing and cranking out cash, other than reading its quarterly and annual reports. You sleep better, which is, for an investor, extremely valuable.

■ ■ ■

So, how do I know if it is a good business? Investors can learn a tremendous amount about the quality of the business by simply looking at its historical financial statements. But looking at the financial statements from one year isn't enough. We should look at the financial statements of companies for at least one business cycle to see how the business has done during good times and bad. You can find the historical financial data of every company that is traded in the United States and in other countries on GuruFocus.com. We compile the historical financial data specifically for this purpose.

Of course, the requirement of at least one business cycle will exclude many companies that have short histories, or new IPOs. Investors should avoid new companies that haven't yet proven themselves.

Don't worry about missing the Next New Thing. Avoiding mistakes and danger zones is more important for long-term investment performance.

To see if a company qualifies as a good company, investors need to ask themselves three fundamental questions while consulting the historical financial statements of companies:

1. Is the company consistently profitable at decent and stable profit margins, through good times and bad?
2. Is this an asset-light business that has a high return on investment capital?
3. Is the company continuously growing its revenue and earnings?

I will now expand upon each of the three questions.

1. Is the company consistently profitable at decent and stable profit margins, through good times and bad?

Just as Lynch said with "earnings, earnings, earnings," people may bet the hourly wiggles in the market, but it's the earnings that waggle the wiggles, long term.[1] "Demonstrated consistent earning power" is also an essential requirement that Buffett expects from the companies he might acquire.

If the company can consistently make money, its intrinsic value will steadily increase. Shareholders are rewarded through the growth of the business, share buybacks, or dividends. The value increases have a great impact on stock prices, too, because over a long period, price always follows value.

The table below shows the performances of the 454 companies of the S&P 500 companies that have been traded from July 2006 through July 2016. The first column is the number of years a company has been profitable, from fiscal year 2006 through 2015. The second column is the number of companies that were profitable during those same years. The third column is the average annualized gain of the stocks over the past ten years. The fourth and fifth columns are the number and percentage of stocks that are still losing money after ten years.

Years of Profitability (2006–2015)	# of Companies	Average Annualized Gain %	# of Stock Losers	% of Stock Losers
10	291	11.1	6	2%
9	88	7.1	15	17%
8	32	6.6	9	28%
7	20	4.4	7	35%
6	12	0.8	4	33%
5	8	4.5	3	38%
4	1	42.8	0	0%
3	0			
2	1	–0.6	1	100%
1	1	4.2	0	0%

From the table above, we can clearly discern a correlation between the company's profitability and its stock performance. Out of the 454 companies that were traded for the last ten years, 291 or 64 percent were profitable every fiscal year from 2006 to 2015. On average, they delivered an annualized return of 11.1 percent a year over the ten-year period. The next group, which was profitable nine out of the ten years, had an average annualized gain of 7.1 percent, which underperformed the first group by a significant 4 percent a year. At the same time, only six stocks, or 2 percent in the first group, had a negative return through the ten years, while 17 percent of stocks in the second group lost money for those who held it for ten years. The next group included those that were profitable eight out of the past ten years and had an annualized average gain of 6.6 percent; 28 percent of the stocks lost money during the ten-year holding period. Again, it underperformed the second group and had more losses. The trend continues.

Therefore, if investors stick to companies that consistently make money, the chance of losing money is greatly diminished. The average gain is much higher.

One may wonder why the gain in the table above is higher than the gain of the S&P 500 Index over the past ten years. There are several deviations for this study from the Index itself:

- The constituent companies of the S&P 500 changed many times over the ten years while in the calculation they do not.
- No rebalance is involved in the calculation.
- All the stocks are initially equal weighted.

I have performed an additional calculation for all the U.S. companies that have been traded in the U.S. market over the past ten years. The results are represented in the table below:

Years of Profitability (2006–2015)	# of Companies	Average Annualized Gain %	# of Stock Losers	% of Stock Losers
10	1045	8.5	61	6%
9	466	4.2	96	21%
8	331	2.7	100	30%
7	285	0.8	91	32%
6	288	−1.4	99	34%
5	306	−0.7	88	29%
4	256	−3.3	83	32%
3	208	−2.9	68	33%
2	188	−4.2	55	29%
1	204	−7	79	39%

The conclusion is essentially the same as for the S&P 500 companies. There have been 3,577 companies traded continuously over the past ten years. Among these 3,577 stocks, 1,045 or 29 percent were able to make money every year. Collectively they averaged an annualized gain of 8.5 percent a year, doubling the gain of 4.2 percent generated by the second group, which were profitable in nine of the ten years. For the companies that were profitable six or fewer years over the past ten, the average gain is negative, even if held for ten years. Overall, the companies that are in the S&P 500 list did better than the average. The overall trend is highlighted in Figure 3.2.

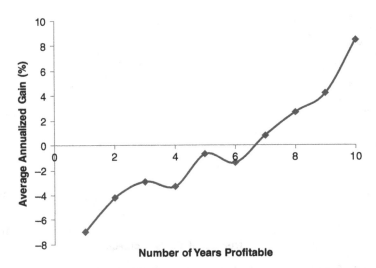

Figure 3.2   Gain vs. Years of Profitability for the U.S. Companies

The possibility of losing money with any stock is greatly diminished for a company that is consistently profitable. The companies that were profitable over the ten years had a 6 percent chance of losing investors' money while the companies that were profitable nine out of the ten years had a 21 percent incidence of losing money. The trend continues, as is evident in Figure 3.3.

One may question whether the study is survival-biased because it only considers the companies that were traded ten years ago and are still traded today. Yes, it is survival-biased, but it is also heavily biased toward the companies that have been losing money. Those that continued to lose money and went bankrupt are not included. If they had been, the gain for the companies that lost money would be even smaller and the percentage of the companies that lost money would be even greater. As an example, SandRidge Energy, the company mentioned in Chapter 1, lost money in six out of the past ten years and has gone bankrupt and therefore has been delisted, but it is not counted toward the loss in the above table. The ones that kept making money but are no longer traded are delisted, mostly as a result of being acquired at a premium to the market price. Again, it proves that time is a friend of the good business and an enemy of the mediocre.

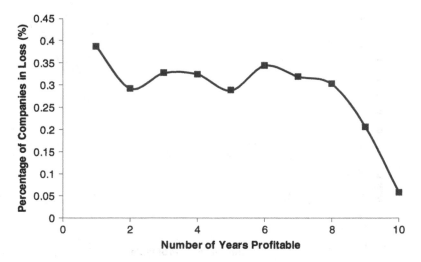

Figure 3.3   % of Companies in Loss vs. Years of Profitability

By simply investing only in the companies that are always profitable, investors can avoid losses and achieve above-average returns.
But we cannot predict the future. Even if a company has always been
profitable, that doesn't mean it will continue to be, which is why we
want to invest in those that consistently have above-average profit
margins. If a company can maintain a higher profit margin over
the long term, it most likely has an economic moat that protects its
pricing power from competition. A higher profit margin also leaves
room for the business to stay profitable during bad times, when a
low and unstable profit-margin business may fall into loss, which
usually results in major punishment to its stock price.

A good question is what kind of profit margin is considered high.
Figure 3.4 reflects the distribution of the operating margins (trailing
12 months of June 2016) of the 3,577 companies referenced earlier.

Many companies have an operating margin between 3 and
8 percent. The median is 10 percent. Roughly 29 percent of companies have an operating margin higher than 20 percent; 16 percent of
companies have a profit margin of 30 percent or higher; 12 percent
of companies have been profitable and have a 10-year median
operating margin higher than 20 percent over the past ten years.

Therefore, if we apply our requirement of consistent profitability
with a 10-year operating margin of 20 percent, only 429, or 12 percent,
of the companies in the United States qualify. That is actually quite a

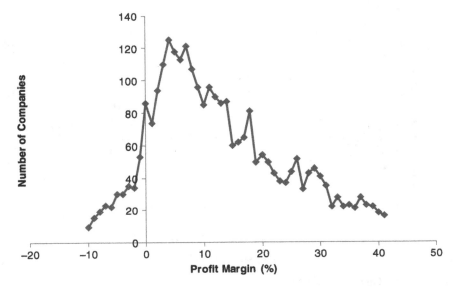

Figure 3.4   Profit Margin Distribution

few. We will ask more questions about these companies and thereby eliminate many of them.

Interestingly, as long as a company was consistently profitable over the ten years, the absolute value of the operating margin didn't make a statistical difference on its stock performance over the past decade. As shown in Figure 3.5, for the 1,045 companies that were consistently profitable over the past ten years, there is no clear correlation between the average annualized gain of the stock and the median operating margin over the same ten-year period.

The consistency of the operating margin is more important than its absolute number. But we still prefer those with higher margins because a lower profit margin leaves less room for error.

As an example, the table below gives the ten-year history of operating margins of Apple, Costco Wholesale, and Alcoa:

Fiscal Year	2006	2007	2008	2009	2010	2011	2012	2013	2014	2015
Apple, Inc.	13	18	19	27	28	31	35	29	29	30
Costco Wholesale	2.70	2.50	2.72	2.49	2.66	2.74	2.78	2.90	2.86	3.12
Alcoa, Inc.	11.93	9.69	2.94	–8.12	2.61	6.01	2.00	–6.03	4.25	3.32

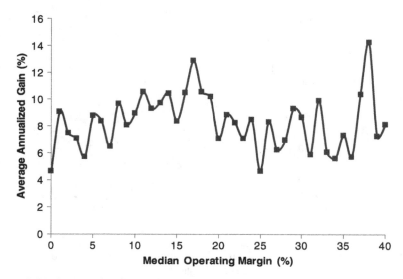

Figure 3.5   Gain vs. Profit Margin

Clearly, Apple has a much higher profit margin than Costco and Alcoa. Though Costco's profit margin is below 3 percent, its margin has been very stable. Its stock averaged more than 13 percent a year over the past ten. Alcoa fell into operating loss in the recessions of 2009 and 2013. After paying interest on its debt, Alcoa lost money in four out of the past ten years. The stock lost 64 percent over the past decade.

Therefore, to determine whether a business is good, consistent profitability is the first and foremost question to answer. Always remember Lynch's earnings, earnings, earnings—businesses are set up to make money. Only those making money can be sustainable. Being able to make money consistently is an essential requirement for a company to qualify as a wonderful business. Isn't this obvious and just common sense?

2. Is this an asset-light business with a high return on investment capital?

If you've ever run a business, you will know how hard it is to run an asset-heavy and capital-intensive business. Starting up is harder, and once the business is running, you continually have to invest a large portion of your earnings into accounts receivable, inventories, and hard assets such as equipment and buildings. You are always tight on cash and must borrow money from time to time to support the expansion of the business.

A friend of mine once ran a small retail business. He kept telling his wife that he had made money from the business. His wife was in doubt and asked him where the money was; in turn, he pointed to the piles of unsold goods in his garage and said, "Here it is."

Such is the situation when you run a capital-intensive business. You don't generate as much cash as your income statement indicates because a large percentage of earnings are reinvested into the business buying and maintaining equipment and increasing inventories. This is required by the business to stay competitive and grow.

It's true that if a business is capital intensive, it is harder for new competitors to come after your market. But it is even better if the business is both light in assets and protected from competition by factors other than capital requirement.

Buffett's own drastically different experiences with the capital-intensive legacy textile business at Berkshire Hathaway and the cash cow See's Candy turned him toward buying asset-light businesses that usually have higher returns on invested capital and employ little debt. He said, "All earnings are not created equal." If an asset-heavy business wants to double its revenue, whether because of inflation or real growth, it has to double the amount of capital tied to inventories and tangible assets. The business has to generate at least the same amount of market value for the amount it reinvested to make it meaningful, which is not often easy to do.

On the other hand, an asset-light business is required to invest less and is positioned to deliver higher real returns to shareholders. An asset-light business can therefore generate higher return on invested capital (ROIC) and higher returns on shareholders' equity (ROE). Because of the light requirement on capital, the company usually employs little debt, unless the management is too aggressive in borrowing to fund growth and acquisitions.

This can be ascertained from the correlation between the average return on invested capital and the percentage of capital expenditure out of the operating cash flow, as shown in Figure 3.6. The chart shows the relationship between the average 10-year median ROIC and the percentage of capex out of operating cash flow for the 3,577 companies discussed earlier. The trend is clear: When a company needs to spend less money out of its operating cash flow, the average return on invested capital is higher.

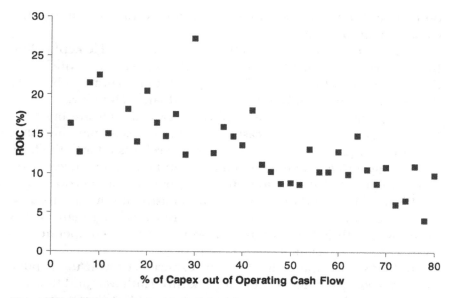

Figure 3.6   ROIC vs. Capex Out of Cashflow

Over the past ten years, very few companies achieved return on invested capital of more than 20 percent, even among companies that are consistently profitable. Figure 3.7 reflects the distribution of the median ROIC over the past ten years for the 1,045 companies that were profitable every single year.

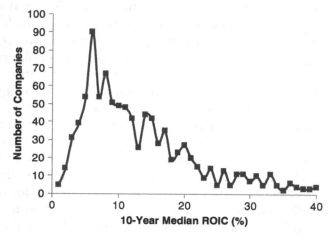

Figure 3.7   ROIC Distribution

The majority of companies have the ten-year median ROIC of less than 15 percent. The peak is at 6 percent. Investors who look for companies that can consistently achieve ROIC of more than 20 percent are searching for diamonds in the rough. Just over 20 percent of the 1,045 companies that were profitable every single year over the past ten years have achieved ROIC over 20 percent.

Not surprisingly, there is a strong correlation between the stock performance and the return on invested capital of companies, even without considering factors such as stock valuation. The relationship of the average gains and the ten-year median ROIC of the 1,045 consistently profitable companies is shown in Figure 3.8.

A similar correlation is found between the performance of stocks and the ten-year median ROE. Figure 3.9 highlights the distribution of the ten-year ROE of the 1,045 companies.

The ROE distribution reflects the same trend as that for ROIC. Very few companies can achieve long-term average ROE of more than 15 percent. Those that did rewarded their shareholders with far above-average returns, as shown in Figure 3.10.

Clearly, if we as investors simply invest in good companies that are consistently profitable and deliver high ROIC and ROE, we would achieve above-average returns. We could achieve this just by buying good companies, and we haven't even mentioned stock valuation.

Back in 2006, the stock market was close to its October 2007 peak for the preceding decade. Today the stock market as a whole is at a similar valuation, as measured by the cycle-adjusted Shiller P/E, and is probably close to another peak. The ten-year period from 2006 to

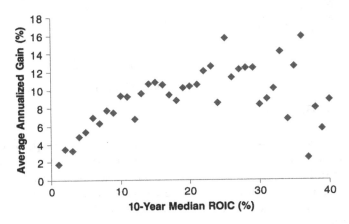

Figure 3.8   Gain vs. ROIC

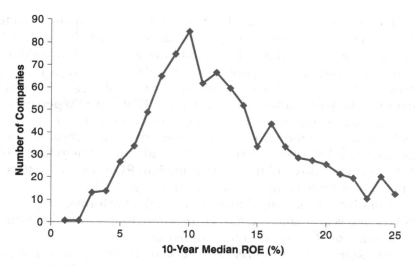

Figure 3.9   ROE Distributions

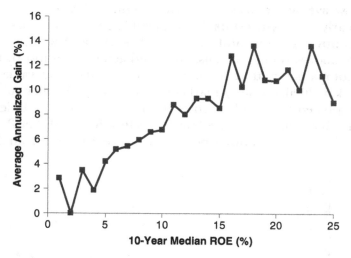

Figure 3.10   Gain vs. ROE

the present is close to a complete market cycle. The outperformance of good companies therefore constitutes convincing evidence that buying good companies will generate above-average returns.

One may argue that this is like looking in the rearview mirror. The fact that the stock of the companies that were consistently profitable and achieved higher returns on invested capital did well in the past ten years does not guarantee that the same kind of stock will continue to perform well. This is true, but if a company is consistently profitable and delivers higher returns, its business value is destined to continuously grow at a faster rate than others. Over a full market cycle, the value will be reflected in its stock price.

Buffett discussed a *Fortune* study that made similar findings in his 1987 shareholder letter.[2] The *Fortune* study found that only 25 of the 1,000 largest companies achieved an average return on equity of over 20 percent in the ten years from 1977 through 1986, and no year worse than 15 percent. "These business superstars were also stock market superstars: During the decade, 24 of the 25 outperformed the S&P 500."

If value goes up, sooner or later price follows. Some things never change, like the laws of physics.

3. Is the company continuously growing its revenue and earnings?

Growth is an extremely important matrix for a good business. If a company can steadily grow its revenue and earnings over the long term while maintaining its profit margin, the company is in an advantageous competitive position within its industry. As a company grows, its fixed cost may not grow as fast; the company will even see its profit margin expand over time. Now it can make even more money on the same amount of goods sold. This is usually the case with asset-light and low-capital-requirement businesses.

Figure 3.11 is the ten-year average earnings-per-share (EPS) growth rate distribution of the 1,045 companies that were profitable through all of the past ten years. We can see that the ten-year average EPS growth rate peaks at about 7 percent a year. The majority of the companies grew their earnings at less than 10 percent a year. Among those 1,045 companies, more than 13 percent had negative EPS growth over the past ten years, although they have always been profitable. Only about 15 percent of companies can grow faster than 15 percent a year.

It is obvious that a faster-growing company can grow its business value faster than a company that is growing slowly. Its stock should do better, too, if everything else is the same. This is exactly the case for the group. Figure 3.12 shows the correlation between the ten-year average gains of the stock and the ten-year average EPS growth rate for the 1,045 consistently profitable companies.

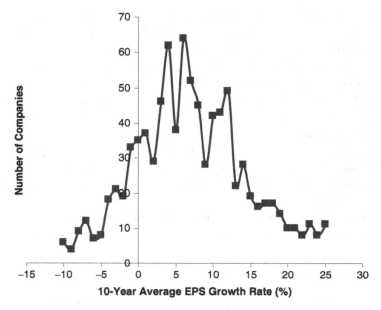

Figure 3.11   Growth Distribution

There is a positive correlation between the rate of EPS growth and the stock performance of the companies. Those that were profitable over the past ten years but had declining EPS did the worst. The stock of the companies that grew 20 percent a year outperformed those that grew 5 percent a year by more than 6 percent on average. The advantage in investing in faster-growing companies is significant. As a group, the faster-growing companies represent a better place to look for better-performing stocks.

Here's an interesting observation from the chart: If the stock of two companies had the same price-to-earnings (P/E) ratio ten years ago, but Company A grows at 5 percent per year and Company B grows at 20 percent per year, and their stock still has the same P/E today, Company B's stock would have outperformed by exactly the same outperformance in the growth of the earnings, which is 15 percent per year. But the 15 percent outperformance in earnings was translated to only about half of that in outperformance of stocks, as is evident in the chart in Figure 3.12. The difference is caused by the shrinkage of P/E for faster-growing companies over the ten years. Very few companies can keep growing at a 20 percent rate for decades. P/E shrinkage is usually what a fast-growing company faces when its growth prospect gets bleaker.

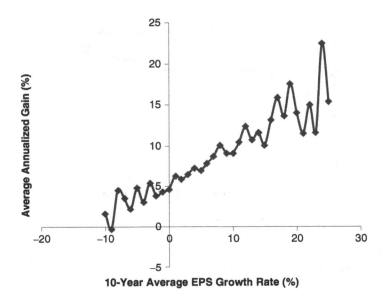

Figure 3.12   Gain vs. Growth

In addition to the growth rate, the consistency of the growth itself plays into the performance of the stock. In 2008, GuruFocus conducted a study and found that if a company could grow its earnings more consistently, its stock did better. Based on the consistency of the revenue and earnings growth, GuruFocus assigned each company a predictability ranking. We repeated the study today and found similar results. The results of the two studies are shown in Figure 3.13. Those with more consistent revenue and earnings growth can outperform those with less consistent growth by as much as 5 percent per year over the ten-year period. Therefore, it is more rewarding to buy companies that can grow consistently and at a faster rate.

■ ■ ■

Now we return to the three fundamental questions. The answers should echo the example I offer ahead for a company to qualify as a good company that we want to buy:

Question 1. Is the company consistently profitable at decent and stable profit margins, through good times and bad?

Answer: Yes. The company has been profitable every single year of the past ten. Its operating margin has been quite stable at double digits, even during the recession and throughout the last industry slowdown.

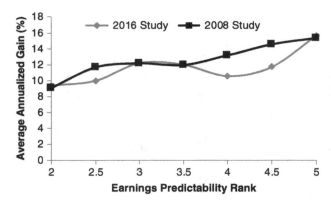

Figure 3.13   Gain vs. Predictability

Question 2. Is this an asset-light business that has a high return on investment capital?

Answer: Yes. This is a capital-light business that on average uses only 30 percent of its operating cash flow for capital expenditure. It is also a high-return business with ROIC of more than 20 percent and ROE of more than 15 percent.

Question 3. Is the company continuously growing its revenue and earnings?

Answer: Yes. The company has been growing its EPS at double digits per year over the past ten years and its growth was consistent, even during recessions and an industry slowdown.

Now we have *yes* answers to all three questions. We have found a company that has demonstrated great past business performance. Before we invest in the company, however, we still need to answer a fourth, more important question about the nature of the business:

4. What is in the nature of the business that has made the company do well in the past?

Will the business continue to do as well as before? The investment returns for those who buy the stock today are much more related to how the company will do in the future than in the past. Baseball Hall of Famer Yogi Berra once said, "It's tough to make predictions, especially about the future." But much like when predicting human behavior in psychology, the best predictor of future behavior is *past behavior*. A company that did well consistently in the past is much more likely to do well in the future than those that didn't previously do well. A company's past success is more likely due to its business nature than other reasons.

We need to answer these questions about the nature of the business: Can the company continue to produce the same or similar products, or provide the same or a similar service in the next five or ten years? Can it grow by simply replicating what it has been doing on a larger scale? What is protecting its pricing power?

We prefer companies that grow just by continuing to do what they have been doing, and on a larger scale. This is Buffett's observation, as he wrote in his 1987 Berkshire Hathaway shareholder letter:

> Experience, however, indicates that the best business returns are usually achieved by companies that are doing something quite similar today to what they were doing five or ten years ago.[3]

If a company continues to produce the similar product, it has the opportunity to continuously improve efficiency, gain more experience, and get better at doing so than everyone else. It also has the time to build the brand and name recognition, and even cultivate taste habits and addictions. Over time, the company can build an economic moat that is hard for others to invade and maintain its high returns.

It is even better if the product or service seems unexciting and has a short consumer purchase cycle. Again, think of consumer staples such as toothpaste, baking soda, and condoms. Consumers are used to the brand or taste and don't compare when they buy. The purchase habits also give the companies tremendous pricing power. These businesses are boring and unsexy, just as Buffett noted about the 25 *Fortune* business superstars in 1987:

> The companies are in businesses that, on balance, seem rather mundane. Most sell non-sexy products or services in much the same manner as they did ten years ago (though in larger quantities now, or at higher prices, or both). Berkshire's experience has been similar. Our managers have produced extraordinary results by doing rather ordinary things—but doing them exceptionally well.[4]

With a company whose products are quickly changing, it is much easier for a new player to come in and do better. Constant changes create opportunities for newcomers. The new players are usually smaller and led by smart and ambitious people. They can make decisions quickly and are willing to take risks. Think of the smartphone market. Apple never produced phones when BlackBerry was the king of the smartphone market. Tesla didn't exist 13 years ago, but now it has the biggest market share in the electric car market and has the reputation of producing the sexiest car in the world. Buffett wrote:

> But a business that constantly encounters major change also encounters many chances for major error. Furthermore, economic terrain that is forever shifting violently is ground on which it is difficult to build a fortress-like business franchise. Such a franchise is usually the key to sustained high returns.[5]

So far I have only referenced the quality of the business—the essential factor to consider when investing in a company. Without quality, there is no need for further consideration.

The quality of a business is just like love in a marriage. As noted in the story in the beginning of the chapter, without love, many more things need to be right to make things work. These things constitute the areas that I have not touched on and include the roles of management, the financial strength of the company, and the valuation of the stock. It is not that they aren't important. They are, but only secondary to the quality of business. They are usually less of a problem for a quality business. I will now discuss these factors in more detail.

Management

Management can make a difference to the operations of the business. But it is even better if the business is immune to the quality of the management and an idiot can run it. These are the businesses that have the economic moat to protect themselves from mistakes or are relatively inert to management decisions. Think Moody's or McDonald's.

The success of a business is much more dependent on the nature of the business than on who runs it. Those that require the best managers are usually not there for the long term "because sooner or later any idiot probably is going to be running it."[6]

An individual investor and minor shareholder rarely has the resources to intimately know the management of a company. The results of operations are mostly decided by the nature of the business rather than management. Buffett likened a poor business to a leaking boat, or a broken car, or a lame horse. It will not do well no matter who rows it, drives it, or rides it. He wrote:

> My conclusion from my own experiences and from much observation of other businesses is that a good managerial record (measured by economic returns) is far more a function of what business boat you get into than it is of how effectively you row (though intelligence and effort help considerably, of course, in any business, good or bad).[7]

I cannot agree more.

Financial Strength

Robust financial strength is of course essential for a company's long-term survivability. Investors may incur permanent loss of capital with those that have weak financial strength. A consistently profitable company with high returns usually generates a lot more cash flow than it needs to grow and doesn't need to borrow money. Naturally it has great financial strength.

You can see this from Figures 3.14 and 3.15. Each point on these charts represents a company, showing where the company is on the map of interest coverage ratio vs. ten-year median return on invested

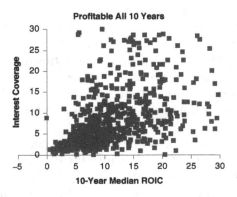

Figure 3.14   Interest Coverage Profitable 10y

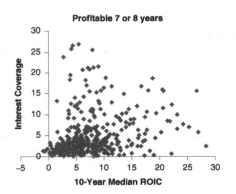

Figure 3.15   Interest Coverage Profitable 7/8y

capital. Figure 3.14 is for the companies that were consistently profitable over the ten years while Figure 3.15 is for the companies that were profitable seven or eight years out of the ten. Clearly, a smaller percentage of the companies on Figure 3.14 has an interest coverage ratio less than 5. Many of the companies on Figure 3.14 have little debt or no debt, and their interest coverage ratio went off the chart and as such they are not displayed. The same isn't true for the companies on Figure 3.15.

For both charts, if the ten-year median ROIC is higher than 15 percent, very few companies have an interest coverage of less than 5. A consistently profitable company with high returns automatically has a strong balance sheet and financial strength.

Valuation

Valuation is of course extremely important to the overall investment return of investors. The portion you overpay for the stock directly reduces your return by the same amount. But buying a consistently profitable and high-return company and holding it for the long term is more forgiving to your initial valuation. An initial overpay of 20 percent is translated to 1.8 percent a year in underperformance if the holding time is ten years, and 6.2 percent a year if the holding time is three years.

A consistently profitable and high-return company also deserves a higher valuation than others because it can grow its intrinsic value faster. Assume we have two companies that both had intrinsic values of $100 per share ten years ago. Company A grows its intrinsic value at 10 percent per year while Company B grows at 18 percent per year.

Ten years later, Company A has a per-share intrinsic value of $259 while Company B has $523. Assume that the market recognized that Company B was a better company ten years ago and gave it a much higher valuation; we bought Company A at $50 per share, which was a 50 percent discount on its intrinsic value, and bought Company B at $100 per share, which was fully valued. After ten years, Company B lost its favor in the market, and both companies are now sold at a 50 percent discount on their intrinsic values. Investors would achieve about the same return from the two investments, which is 10 percent per year over the past ten years, although they paid twice the price for Company B.

If ten years ago the market gave investors the opportunity to buy Company B at $70 instead of $100, the annualized return with Company B would be 14.1 percent a year. Although investors still paid Company B a 40 percent higher price than with Company A for the same intrinsic value, the investment with Company B rewarded investors with an additional 4.1 percent a year for ten years because Company B is a better business and grew its intrinsic value faster.

It would be ideal if we could buy Company B at a 50 percent discount on its intrinsic value, too. But the stock market usually gives higher valuations to better companies. However, it is still worthwhile to pay up for a good business.

This serves as mathematical proof of the Buffett philosophy that it is far better to buy good companies at fair prices than fair companies at good prices.

■ ■ ■

Charlie Munger said: "The difference between a good business and a bad business is that good businesses throw up one easy decision after another. The bad businesses throw up painful decisions time after time."[8] Good businesses offer investors the opportunity to make easier decisions and also fewer decisions.

All things considered, buying good businesses that are consistently profitable, generating high returns, and growing is paramount. With good companies, other circumstances will take care of themselves.

So, buy only good companies!

4

Again, Buy Only Good Companies—and Know Where to Find Them

"Keep it simple."

—Charlie Munger

I reiterate the title from Chapter 3 because if there is one thing you should remember from reading this book, it is to buy only good companies!

It isn't that other companies won't make you money. They may make you a lot of money. Donald Yacktman didn't buy Chrysler because the auto industry was not the place he wanted to be, not because Chrysler wouldn't make him money. If you buy only good companies, your chance of making money is much improved and the journey is far more pleasant.

Peter Lynch can make money anywhere; he knows about every industry and how to succeed in every investing situation, and he owns thousands of stocks. But you don't have to be like Lynch; as Charlie Munger said: "You don't have to know everything. A few really big ideas carry most of the freight."[1]

A woman calls in a plumber when her washing machine breaks down. The plumber arrives, studies the machine, then takes out a hammer and gives it a hefty whack. The washing machine starts working again, and the plumber presents her with a bill for $200. "Two hundred dollars?" says the woman. "All you did was hit it with the hammer." So, the plumber presents her with an itemized bill: *Hitting washing machine with a hammer: $5. Knowing where to hit it: $195.*

This joke has been used in many situations to enlighten people on how, and where, to focus their effort. When it comes to investing, buy only good companies! The advice seems simple, but it is not always easy to follow—numerous opportunities in the market pose appealing gains.

As mentioned in Chapter 1, Lynch categorized investment opportunities into six classes.[2] I will examine them all and demonstrate whether the idea of buying only good companies applies to each.

Asset Plays

An asset play is the situation that occurs when a company is sitting on something valuable, but this is not reflected in its stock price. These days, the valuable assets are often understated real estate. This refers to the deep-bargain investing where the stock price is much lower compared to the asset value, net current asset value, or net-net working capital of the business, as I examined in Chapter 2. Unless the situation is extremely liquid and takes a short time to liquidate, or the business itself is decent and generates enough cash flow to be self-sustaining, investors should avoid investing in asset plays altogether.

Warren Buffett calls it "foolish." Yacktman likens it to a factory that is idle but the machines can be cheaply bought. Remember Sears? As this writing progresses, Sears is still "unlocking value." But, "It's taking much longer than we thought," as Bruce Berkowitz admitted in his 2016 semiannual shareholder letter,[3] published July 28, 2016, and which can be translated into "It is eroding more value than we thought." *Avoid asset plays.*

Turnarounds

Turnarounds are the companies that "have been battered, depressed and often can barely drag themselves into Chapter 11."[4] Lynch made many multibaggers from turnarounds. Above all, the stock price was usually badly beaten down and the recovery could be strong from the rock-bottom levels. But Lynch also has a long list of turnarounds he wishes he'd never bought.

Avoid investing in turnarounds. The mere fact that the company could get itself into trouble precludes it from qualifying as a good company. And these problems rarely go away, as Buffett wrote in his

1979 shareholder letter, suffering from the pain of trying to turn the embattled textile business around:

> Both our operating and investment experience cause us to conclude that "turnarounds" seldom turn, and that the same energies and talent are much better employed in a good business purchased at a fair price than in a poor business purchased at a bargain price.[5]

We witnessed a high-profile turnaround effort at JC Penney a few years ago. Under the direction of corporate raider and activist investor Bill Ackman, former Apple store genius Ron Johnson was brought in to turn the business around. But Johnson couldn't replicate the magic he performed at Apple, and the turnaround effort failed spectacularly. Ackman lost 60 percent on his billion-dollar investment in JC Penney and gave up.

Still struggling to turn the textile business around, Buffett wrote in his 1980 shareholder letter:[6]

> We have written in past reports about the disappointments that usually result from purchase and operation of "turnaround" businesses. Literally hundreds of turnaround possibilities in dozens of industries have been described to us over the years and, either as participants or as observers, we have tracked performance against expectations. Our conclusion is that, with few exceptions, when a management with a reputation for brilliance tackles a business with a reputation for poor fundamental economics, it is the reputation of the business that remains intact.

That is exactly what happened to the reputation of Ron Johnson, who succeeded at Apple but not at JC Penney. Above all, Apple is Apple—and JC Penney is just JC Penney.

But didn't Buffett make a killing with the turnaround of GEICO? He paid $45.7 million in 1976–1979 for one-third of the company, which was eventually worth $2.3 billion when he acquired the remaining shares of GEICO. In the early 1970s, the executives running GEICO made some serious errors in estimating their claims costs, a mistake that led the company to underprice its policies, which almost caused it to go bankrupt.

Though in trouble, GEICO's fundamental competitive strength was unchanged, according to Buffett, and is the reason he bought GEICO. He explained in his 1980 letter:[7]

> GEICO's problems at that time put it in a position analogous to that of American Express in 1964 following the salad oil scandal. Both were one-of-a-kind companies, temporarily reeling from the effects of a fiscal blow that did not destroy their exceptional underlying economics. The GEICO and American Express situations, extraordinary business franchises with a localized excisable cancer (needing, to be sure, a skilled surgeon), should be distinguished from the true "turnaround" situation in which the managers expect—and need—to pull off a corporate Pygmalion.

Therefore, the most important test to distinguish a true "turnaround" from the "localized excisable cancer" is if the business still has the "fundamental competitive strength" and "exceptional underlying economics" it once enjoyed. If we apply this to Sears and JC Penney, we can clearly see that they don't. So much for their turnarounds.

Investors should also distinguish a market manipulation from a true turnaround, as both can result in the collapse of stock prices. This happened to Fairfax Financial, a Canadian insurance company founded by value investor Prem Watsa, who got into the insurance business under the influence of Buffett. Watsa became a successful value investor after studying Benjamin Graham and John Templeton. Under his leadership, Fairfax had grown its book value by more than 20 percent a year since 1985. In 2004–2005, Fairfax was traded in both the United States and Canada at around $200 a share, when it became the target of influential short sellers. Fairfax was compared to the infamous accounting manipulator and then-bankrupt company Enron. Fairfax stock lost 50 percent of its market value and dropped to $100 a share. Fairfax then sued the short sellers and withdrew its stock from trading in the U.S. market. The dust finally settled and Fairfax continued to grow its book value at a 20 percent annual rate, and it made a killing during the financial crisis in 2008 by shorting the stock market. Now Fairfax is traded at around $700 as of October 2016.

Fairfax's trouble came from stock manipulations. The short sellers' attacks damaged its reputation, which may have temporarily affected its insurance business. But its business was doing fine, and the short sellers in fact created a great buying opportunity for long-term investors.

In conclusion, turnarounds seldom turn and shouldn't be considered good companies. An investor can, however, find many good opportunities; the key is to identify the companies that are in trouble but still have "fundamental competitive strength" and "exceptional underlying economics." *Avoid true turnarounds!*

Cyclicals

A cyclical business sees the demand for its products expand and contract periodically every several years. The demand is often synchronized with the economic cycle. The business usually requires high capital investment and heavy fixed assets. Its production capacity cannot expand quickly when demand is high and cannot be eliminated when demand is low. The business tends to invest to expand its production capacity when demand is strong, but when the production capacity is ready, the demand has already dwindled, resulting in a dramatic decline in profit and heavy debt.

Highly cyclical industries include auto, airline, steel, oil and gas, chemicals, and many others. Sometimes a cyclical business can ride on a tailwind and expand for many years, disguising it as secular growth. For instance, the housing industry, which was driven by declining interest rates, expanded almost ten years before its collapse.

Cyclical industries are not the places in which to find good companies for a long-term hold. Yacktman didn't want to buy Chrysler because the auto industry is too cyclical. Investors should also stay away from cyclical industries.

Although Howard Marks said, "most things will prove to be cyclical,"[8] some industries are definitely more cyclical than others. A way to identify a cyclical industry is to see how its sales and profit did over at least ten years, and especially during recessions. An example is reflected in Figure 4.1.

This chart shows the net income of CVS Health Corp. and Dow Chemical. The gray areas in the chart denote the periods in which the U.S. economy was in recession. Dow Chemical's net income dropped drastically during these recessions. In the 2002 recession, Dow Chemical fell into loss; in the 2008 recession, its

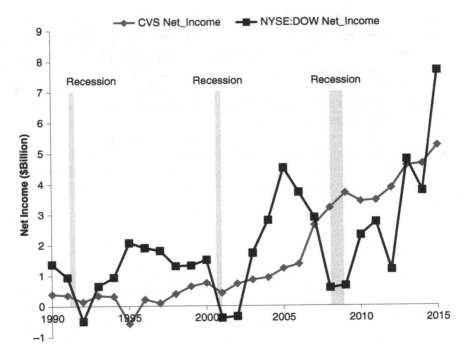

Figure 4.1   CVS DOW Net Income

net income dropped from above $4 billion a year to less than $1 billion—meanwhile, CVS's net income was barely affected by the recessions.

Clearly Dow Chemical is a cyclical business while CVS is not. Holding cyclicals long term is not very rewarding. Holding leveraged cyclicals can be extremely dangerous. Many cyclicals can't outlast recessions, and they go bankrupt. Think of how many bankruptcies we have heard about for carmakers, airlines, mining companies, and oil explorers. By definition, they cannot meet the requirement of long-term and consistent profitability that we have established for good companies. *Avoid cyclicals.*

Slow Growers

Slow growers are mature companies that have lost their growth steam. Their revenue base is too expansive for them to find new markets for growth. Therefore, their revenue is not growing much faster than the economy. Think of Wal-Mart, Microsoft, Procter &

Gamble, and Johnson & Johnson. These companies are usually hugely profitable and have high returns. For the three questions on profitability, return on invested capital, and growth we ask about good companies in the last chapter, we have acceptable answers for Question 1 (long-term, consistent profitability) and Question 2 (high return on invested capital), but not for Question 3 (double-digit growth).

The investment returns from the stock of slow growers can be satisfactory if bought at lower valuations relative to their historical mean. Slow growers are a good choice for steady and high dividends when building an income portfolio. I will discuss more about this in Chapter 8.

The Stalwarts

The stalwarts are typically midsized companies that are growing at a low double-digit rate and still have exceptional potential ahead of them. They represent the ideal field in which to find good companies that have long-term profitability, high return, and double-digit growth. The companies are growing at decent rates and have proven track records. Holding these stocks can be unexciting, but holding high-quality companies over the long term has little investment risk, which can be very rewarding.

A stalwart company may grow slower in one year and faster in another. We look at the long-term average of the business performance in the areas of growth, profitability, and business returns. We need to analyze what caused the company to grow slower than in the past and see if the slower growth will become the norm for the future. Sometimes industry transformation destroys the economic moat the business once enjoyed, or the business itself deviates from its past track under existing or new management. Investors need to continue to watch the growth and profitability of these companies. No business is perfect or hiccup-free.

I have created a good companies screen in GuruFocus's All-In-One Screener for readers to find these companies. Simply go to GuruFocus.com → All-In-One Screener → GuruFocus Screens → The Good Companies. I have also created a portfolio that monitors the performance of the stocks that appear on the screener as of August 2016.

With this screener, we find companies such as AutoZone, AMETEK Inc., and Jack Henry & Associates Inc. These are steady and profitable growers with high return on invested capital and the potential for more growth. Their stocks also did extremely well during the past decade.

Lynch sells the stalwarts after a gain of 50 percent in a year or two. But they can also be long-term steady growers. It is often worthwhile to hold them for the long term, as selling will result in capital gain tax and missed opportunities to buy these high-quality companies again. Consider AutoZone. There has never been a good time to sell AutoZone. The company has been growing its revenue at about 15 percent a year, year in and year out, and even during recessions. Holding it for the long term has been extremely rewarding.

Fast Growers

Fast growers are the companies that grow at above 20 percent. They are usually small and aggressive new companies. This is Lynch's favorite land, where he found many ideas that eventually gained 10 times, 20 times, and more.

As Lynch pointed out, the fast growers don't have to be in a fast-growing industry. Ideally, they are the companies that grab market shares from existing players. While the reward can be great, the risk in investing in fast growers can also be high. The fast growers may grow too fast and get into too much debt. The high expectations of Wall Street usually elevate their valuations to fragile levels. Any hiccup in growth will result in severe punishment to their stocks.

Enter Chipotle Mexican Grill. The fast-food chain grew its revenue by more than 20 percent per year on average for the past decade. Its stock was trading at P/E of above 50 in 2014, as the company seemed unstoppable, opening more stores and enjoying double-digit same-store sales growth. Then, in 2015 the restaurant chain was hit by a virus and facing federal investigation. The same-store sales are now in decline, and the stock has lost close to 50 percent from its peak in 2015.

It is hard to find good companies that have proven themselves over the long term in the land of fast growers, as these companies usually don't have enough history. Some of them, however, over time can develop into the good companies we are looking for.

■ ■ ■

In summary, as investors are looking to buy only good companies, we will not consider asset plays, cyclicals, and turnarounds from among Lynch's six categories. We may barely find qualified companies among slow growers and fast growers—the best ones are the stalwarts. The stalwarts are more likely to meet the good companies' requirements. Again, these requirements are:

1. Long-term and consistent profitability
2. High business returns as measured by high return on invested capital and high return on equity
3. Above-average growth

If you are a plumber, know where to hit.

The Cyclicity of Businesses

The cyclicity of businesses deserves further consideration. It is one of the first things Yacktman looks at in a business. He prefers businesses with a long product cycle and short consumer purchase cycle, which means businesses that are not cyclical. As pointed out by Marks, most things are cyclical, as illustrated in the net income of different sectors in the following. At the bottoms of the cycles, demand for the products slows. A small decline in sales can translate into huge drops in the profits of the business because the cost cannot be reduced as quickly as the demand, and the reduction of the cost itself costs money.

Because of the nature of business, some industries can never produce consistently good returns for their shareholders. Buying good companies means avoiding these industries altogether. I have mentioned cyclical industries such as autos, airlines, chemicals, steel, and energy. I now want to examine in further detail the cyclicity of certain businesses.

The basic materials sector is one of those. Figure 4.2 illustrates the history of the total revenue of the 732 U.S. companies that are currently traded in the basic materials sector. These include companies in the industries of agriculture, building materials, chemicals, coal, forest products, metals, and mining.

We can see that during the years 1992, 1998, 2002, 2008, and 2015, the revenue for basic materials declined. Among those years, 1992, 2002, and 2008 are associated with recessions. The total revenue of these companies shrank from previous years by a few

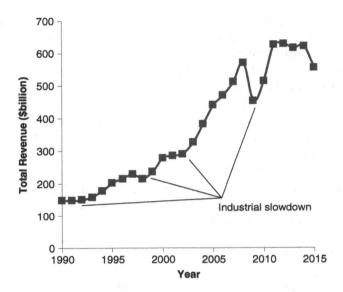

Figure 4.2   Basic Materials Revenue

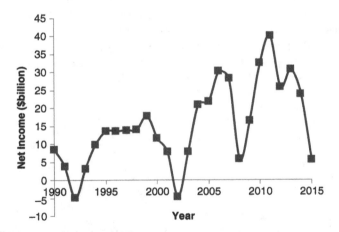

Figure 4.3   Basic Materials Net Income

percent most of the time because even in the good years, 1999, 2006, and 2010, the sector had an average profit margin of just above 6 percent. The insignificant few percent of decline in revenue resulted in dramatic collapses in the total profit of the sector, as is evident in Figure 4.3.

During the years 1992 and 2002, the basic materials sector fell into deep loss. In the years 2008 and 2015, the sector gave up more than 80 percent of profits in relation to previous years and was barely profitable as a whole. The capital- and asset-intensive nature of the sector makes it hard to quickly adjust cost as demand slows. The products in the business are usually commodities, making it hard for businesses to raise prices to compensate for the loss in demand. These factors make the basic materials businesses highly cyclical.

Shareholders in this sector usually find that their companies swing wildly between profit and loss every several years. Many companies cannot pass the test of bad times and go bankrupt. As Buffett said, "In a business selling a commodity-type product, it's impossible to be a lot smarter than your dumbest competitor."[9] So companies must compete on prices, and they have similar patterns of profit and loss. They just cannot generate consistent earnings over a long period.

Therefore, companies producing agricultural products, building materials, chemicals, coal, forest products, and metals are not good businesses. Lynch once said that companies selling commodity-like products should come with a warning label: "Competition may prove hazardous to human wealth." Avoid them!

Similar behavior is observed in the energy and consumer cyclical sectors. Their profits are reflected in Figures 4.4 and 4.5. As we

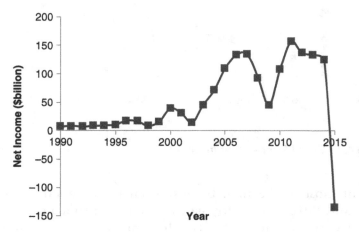

Figure 4.4   Energy Net Income

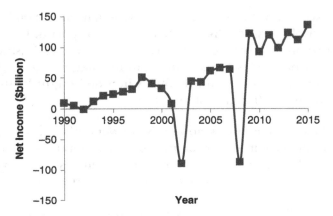

Figure 4.5   Consumer Cyclical Net Income

can see, the consumer cyclicals sector is indeed cyclical. This sector includes industries such as auto, entertainment, manufacturing, travel and leisure, and luxury goods. These always experience deep losses during recessions. It is hard to build consistently profitable companies in these industries.

For the technology sector, the behaviors of hardware and software businesses are quite different. The hardware producers, such as telecom equipment and computer companies, are more asset-heavy and capital-intensive. Thus, these are more susceptible to economic cycles. Because of the continuous changes in technology, it is difficult for a hardware business to stay competitive over the long term.

But some software companies have developed products and services in areas that don't change as fast. For example, Microsoft and Google have built their economic moats and have become great companies with consistent earnings power and a high return on invested capital and growth. A company called Ansys Inc. makes simulation software that is widely used in industries from aerospace, defense, auto, and construction to healthcare, energy, and almost everything else. The software needs to be tested and verified repeatedly in the real production world. Once the software is found reliable, no customer will want to risk changing to new software from another company; thus, Ansys has established its moat.

Banking didn't display much sensitivity to cycles and recessions for almost two decades as the industry rode on the tailwind of housing expansion, until the housing crisis started in 2007. A bank can be a simple business like a small community bank focusing on conservative home mortgages; it can also be a complex business with who knows what on its book. Buffett didn't like banks in general. He didn't buy bank stocks until 1990, when he bought Wells Fargo. He wrote in his 1990 shareholder letter:[10]

> The banking business is no favorite of ours. When assets are twenty times equity—a common ratio in this industry—mistakes that involve only a small portion of assets can destroy a major portion of equity. And mistakes have been the rule rather than the exception at many major banks. Most have resulted from a managerial failing that we described last year when discussing the "institutional imperative": the tendency of executives to mindlessly imitate the behavior of their peers, no matter how foolish it may be to do so. In their lending, many bankers played follow-the-leader with lemming-like zeal; now they are experiencing a lemming-like fate.

This is exactly what led Citigroup into trouble under its former CEO Charles Prince, who famously said about Citigroup's continued commitment to leveraged buyout deals, despite fears of reduced liquidity because of the subprime meltdown: "As long as the music is playing, you've got to get up and dance."

I once heard this joke:

> What do you have to do to become a successful banker? Follow three rules: First, don't lend money to those who can't repay; second, don't lend money to those who need it badly; and third, don't lend your own money.

During the housing craze of the 2000s, most bankers just remembered the third rule.

Buffett considers management the key to a bank. He continued in his 1990 letter:

> Because leverage of 20:1 magnifies the effects of managerial strengths and weaknesses, we have no interest in purchasing shares of a poorly-managed bank at a "cheap" price. Instead, our only interest is in buying into well-managed banks at fair prices.

This is also what Munger echoed in the 2016 shareholder meeting of Daily Journal Inc., for which he serves as chairman:[11]

> I don't think anybody could ever buy a bank who doesn't have a feeling for how really shrewd the management is. Banking is a field where it's easy to delude yourself into reporting big numbers that aren't really being earned. It's a very dangerous place for an investor. Without deep insight into banking, you should [avoid it].

Lynch loves community banks and savings and loans. The business for these small banks is much simpler and conservative bankers can be found within them.

Healthcare and consumer defensive sectors are relatively insensitive to economic cycles. After all, people still go to doctors when they get sick. The consumer defensive sectors include food, drinks, tobaccos, and other low-priced, daily-consumed products. Consumers are not sensitive to the price changes of these products and cannot withhold their purchases even if the prices increase, which gives the pricing power to the companies. These are the products that are consumed daily and therefore have a short consumer purchase cycle, as preferred by Yacktman. On the other hand, the products are usually simple and have a very long life cycle. For example, since Berkshire Hathaway purchased See's Candy in 1972, the company has been making the same kinds of candies. Therefore, the required invested capital is light. This is a field in which many great businesses are built. We as investors can participate in the growth of these businesses and can be rewarded by buying their stocks and holding them for the long term. (See Figures 4.6 and 4.7.)

This is also what renowned value investor Tom Russo has been doing for more than three decades. He put more than 60 percent of his portfolio into food and drink companies like Nestle, Heineken, Anheuser-Busch, and Pernod Ricard, and cigarette companies such as Philip Morris International and its sister company Altria. Buying these high-return and consistently profitable companies bears little risk and imposes no need to sell. His quarterly portfolio turnover is less than 2 percent, and he has achieved an excellent long-term track record.

Investors need to be wary of retailing businesses, though they belong to consumer defensive. This is what Buffett wrote about retailing in his 1995 shareholder letter:[12]

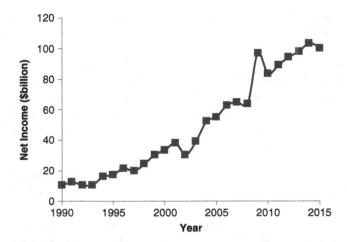

Figure 4.6   Healthcare Net Income

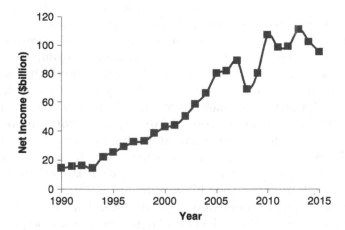

Figure 4.7   Consumer Defensive Net Income

Retailing is a tough business. During my investment career, I have watched a large number of retailers enjoy terrific growth and superb returns on equity for a period, and then suddenly nosedive, often all the way into bankruptcy. This shooting-star phenomenon is far more common in retailing than it is in manufacturing or service businesses. In part, this is because a retailer must stay smart, day after day. Your competitor is always copying and then topping whatever you do. Shoppers are meanwhile beckoned in every conceivable way to try a stream of new merchants. In retailing, to coast is to fail.

In summary, the dedication to buy only good companies means that investors should avoid the companies in the highly cyclical sectors such as basic materials, computer hardware, telecom, and semiconductor companies, no matter how attractive the opportunities appear. The nature of these businesses is simply prohibitive for anyone to build consistently profitable companies. The sectors of consumer defensive and healthcare are almost noncyclical. They represent better places to find great companies with high returns and consistent profitability.

Shooting for the Stars versus Shooting Fish in a Barrel

Sticking to buying good companies also means that we are going to miss some of the best-performing stocks. When I sort the 3,577 companies that were continuously trading for the past ten years by their performances, the best-performing 50 stocks delivered an annualized gain of just under 25 percent or higher. Among the 50 stocks, 6 were in biotech and 5 were in software. These two industries produced most of the star performers in the past ten years. We are not likely to catch any of them because we choose to invest in good companies with great long-term performance records. None of these companies qualified as a good company ten years ago. Even today, very few of them qualify.

Let's first look at the star performers in the biotech industry. The best-performing stock is Medivation Inc. It gained an average of almost 50 percent a year over the past ten years. Ten years ago, the company had no revenue and was losing tens of millions a year. The market cap was already more than $100 million. Why would the market value a company with no revenue at hundreds of millions of dollars? Any sensible investor would not buy the stock. The company went another year without revenue while its market cap grew to more than $400 million. The company did make it, and now it has close to $1 billion in annual revenue and more than $250 million in net income. But it didn't turn a profit until 2014, when its market cap had grown to more than $7 billion. Today the market values the company at more than $10 billion.

How could anyone have spotted such an opportunity ten years ago? How could anyone foresee that the company could grow from no revenue to close $1 billion in ten years? Even with deep knowledge and industry insight, it seems impossible to do. Searching for such an opportunity ten years ago was indeed like shooting for the stars.

Now let's take a look at the second-best biotech stock, BioSpecifics Technologies Corp. Over the past ten years, the company's stock gained 43 percent a year annualized. A decade ago, the company had a tiny market cap of about $5 million. Its revenue shrank from $5.5 million in 2005 to $1.9 million in 2006 and was losing $3.3 million on that. Even today the revenue of the company is a mere $23 million a year. It is making a net profit of $10 million. The market cap is now $284 million. While the gain is attractive, a market cap of only $5 million ten years ago is too small for even many individual investors, and the company was in deep loss in its operations.

In the software industry, the two best-performing stocks were EBIX Inc. and Tyler Technologies. EBIX, an insurance software provider, delivered an average gain of 40 percent. Tyler provides management software for local governments and gained 30 percent a year for the past ten years. EBIX had revenue of under $30 million while Tyler had less than $200 million. They would not be considered good companies in 2006 because both only recently turned profitable. They could not pass the test of long-term consistent profitability found in good companies.

We would also miss other best-performing stocks of the past decade like Amazon.com, Apple, and Priceline for the same reasons. These companies haven't proven themselves for consistent profitability. Does it sound terrible? No, because we also have dodged a much higher probability of loss with many other companies.

Let's consider all the biotech stocks that were traded in the market in 2006. At the beginning of 2006, there were 210 U.S.-based biotech companies that had less than $100 million in annual sales. This includes companies that were later delisted for being acquired or going bankrupt. Sixty-seven, or 32 percent, of these companies went bankrupt in the following years. Another 40 percent of the stocks are still negative, even after a holding period of ten years. These 210 companies have a median gain of negative 80 percent. If we consider the 90 companies that had sales profiles similar to the star performers, such as Medivation and BioSpecifics, 70 percent later went bankrupt; 87 percent of the stocks lost more than 90 percent.

The software industry did somewhat better, although the odds of picking losers still ran extremely high. Among all 357 U.S.-based software companies that had less than $100 million in revenue and were traded in 2006, around 20 percent went bankrupt later. Investors are still losing money—more than 57 percent of them, even after a holding period of ten years. These 357 companies had a median gain of negative 28 percent. What is the chance of picking the star performers among these companies? If you didn't pick the winners, the losers cost you big.

If we look at the companies that would qualify as good companies in 2006, they would have been profitable over the previous ten years and have had a median return on invested capital of more than 20 percent. We found 205 companies at the beginning of 2006. If we held them for ten years, 5 percent of them went bankrupt later. We would have lost money on 31 percent of the companies after ten years. These 205 companies have a much higher median gain of 34 percent. Overall, the chance of losing money is much smaller.

If betting on picking the best performers is like shooting for the stars, buying good companies at fair prices is like shooting fish in a barrel. You may not get the star performers, but you get a lot of decent ones such as retail chain Dollar Tree and baking soda and condom maker Church & Dwight. More importantly, you avoid a lot of deep losses.

Therefore, by buying only good companies, we are focusing on a much better neighborhood of the investing universe. We are trying to eliminate the chance of losing money by buying those that have already proven themselves. We have a much smaller universe than Lynch in picking stocks. We want to stay in the proximity of good companies. We don't want to get into situations where we have high odds of losing money.

Didn't Munger once say: "All I want to know is where I'm going to die so I'll never go there"?

I want to finish this chapter with the wisdom of Buffett:[13]

> What counts for most people in investing is not how much they know, but rather how realistically they define what they don't know. An investor needs to do very few things right as long as he or she avoids big mistakes.

CHAPTER

5

Buy Good Companies at Fair Prices

"Anything worth doing is worth doing slowly."

—Mae West

In the previous two chapters, I examined the kinds of companies that qualify as the "good companies" we will buy and where to find them. But buying good companies itself does not guarantee good results. It works only if they are bought at fair prices. I have asserted that if you buy a good company, there is no risk of permanent loss of capital as long as its business continues to perform well and the company's value keeps growing. But any excess payment above the fair price will eat into your returns.

For example, riding the tide of the stock market bubble, Wal-Mart stock gained more than 500 percent in three years, to around $70 a share by the end of 1999. Then it took 12 years for anyone who bought Wal-Mart stock at the end of 1999 to break even. Even today, Wal-Mart is barely higher than it was 16 years ago. Wal-Mart certainly met the good-company requirement in 1999. It had been always profitable, had a ROIC in the mid-teens, and grew its earnings at double digits. But the problem was that the stock was overvalued. It had a P/E ratio of 60 at the end of 1999. Today, the P/E ratio of the stock is 16. Wal-Mart has quadrupled its earnings from 1999, but those who bought in 1999 have not benefited because they overpaid for the stock.

Another example is Coca-Cola. The stock was traded at $43 (split-adjusted) in the middle of 1998. After 18 years, today the stock is traded at below $43. Coca-Cola is a great company. Warren

Buffett bought it in 1988. Its return on invested capital was above 30 percent in the 1990s. But from the middle of 1998 to today, the stock hasn't done much. The reason is the same as it is for Wal-Mart. The stock was even more overvalued than Wal-Mart's. In the middle of 1998, the stock was traded at the P/E ratio of 95. The only returns investors received over those 18 years are in the form of dividends, which have averaged a dismal 2 percent. The 400 million shares of Coca-Cola that Berkshire Hathaway owns was worth $17 billion 18 years ago. It remains worth that much today.

As a reminder, you can check out the historical P/E ratios and dividend yields and numerous other key statistics using GuruFocus's Interactive Chart.

To some extent, Buffett regretted not selling the overvalued stock later, after the 1999 bubble burst. He wrote in his 2004 shareholder letter:[1]

> Nevertheless, I can properly be criticized for merely clucking about nose-bleed valuations during the Bubble rather than acting on my views. Though I said at the time that certain of the stocks we held were priced ahead of themselves, I underestimated just how severe the overvaluation was. I talked when I should have walked.

Therefore, satisfactory returns can only be achieved if stocks are bought at reasonable prices.

I have previously compared the long-term holding of great companies to marriage. Charlie Munger said that the secret to a happy marriage is to find someone who has low expectations. This applies as well to the investor's marriage to a good company. High expectations from the market create overvaluation, which will not generate pleasant results for those involved.

So, what kind of valuation is fair? There are many ways to evaluate businesses. Each may apply to a different situation, depending on the nature of the business itself. I will discuss the different valuation methods in further detail in Chapter 9. Here, I will focus on the two most common methods: the discounted cash flow model (DCF) and price/earnings (P/E) ratio. Both have limitations and cannot be applied to every situation, but both work quite well for the good companies we want to buy. They are ultimately equivalent in assessing the fair values of businesses.

Discounted Cash Flow Model

The theory of discounted cash flow (DCF) was originated by John Burr Williams in his PhD thesis at Harvard in 1937. It was published in 1938 as a book titled *The Theory of Investment Value.*[2] The theory for the discounted cash flow model can be summarized as: *The value of any stock, bond, or business today is determined by the cash inflows and outflows—discounted at an appropriate interest rate—that can be expected to occur during the remaining life of the asset.*

Therefore, the DCF model is looking into the future. But we know only the past. We have to make some assumptions about the future, though many of these are based on how the business did in the past. These assumptions include:

- The future business growth rate
- The number of years of the business's remaining life
- The discount rate

Assuming the business is currently earning $E(0)$ in free cash flow per year and the business growth rate is g, in n years the business will earn this much:

$$E(n) = E(0)(1 + g)^n$$

After n years, the amount $E(n)$ is not worth as much as the present value of $E(n)$; it has to be discounted to its current value, which is equal to:

$$E(0)(1 + g)^n/(1 + d)^n = E(0)[(1 + g)/(1 + d)]^n$$

where d is the discount rate. If the business can consistently do this for n years, the total earnings over the years will be:

$$E(0)\{(1 + g)/(1 + d) + [(1 + g)/(1 + d)]^2 + [(1 + g)/(1 + d)]^3 + \cdots +$$
$$[(1 + g)/(1 + d)]^n\}$$
$$= E(0)\,x(1-x^n)/(1-x)$$

where $x = (1 + g)/(1 + d)$.

Obviously, no business can grow forever. At some point the growth will slow and then cease. But the business still has its value for as long as it is generating cash for its owners. Therefore, we divide the business into two stages. One is the growth stage; the other is the terminal stage. Assume at the terminal stage that the business growth rate is t after n years of growth at the rate of g. The duration of the terminal stage lasts m years. The terminal value of the business will be:

$$E(0)[(1 + g)/(1 + d)]^n\{(1 + t)/(1 + d) + [(1 + t)/(1 + d)]^2$$
$$+ [(1 + t)/(1 + d)]^3 + \cdots + [(1 + t)/(1 + d)]^m\}$$
$$= E(0)x^n y(1-y^m)/(1-y)$$

where $y = (1 + t)/(1 + d)$.

Putting everything together, as established by the DCF model, the intrinsic value of a business can be calculated using this equation:

Intrinsic Value = Future Earnings at Growth Stage + Terminal Value

Therefore $= E(0)x(1 - x^n)/(1 - x) + E(0)x^n y(1 - y^m)/(1 - y)$, where $x = (1 + g)/(1 + d)$, and $y = (1 + t)/(1 + d)$.

This is the intrinsic value equation based on the discounted earnings. These are the parameters used in the equation:

$E(0)$ = current earnings (Here I don't explicitly distinguish earnings and free cash flow as the formula works for both cases in the same way.)

G = the growth rate at the growth stage

d = the discount rate

t = the growth rate at the terminal stage

n = the number of years at the growth stage

m = the number of years at the terminal stage

GuruFocus has created a two-stage fair value calculator based on the DCF model. We assume by default that the growth rate of the growth stage of the next ten years is equal to its average earnings-per-share growth rate in the previous ten years or 20 percent, whichever is smaller; the growth rate in the terminal stage is 4 percent, which also lasts ten years. We used earnings (without nonrecurring items) per share instead of free cash flow per share for the calculation because our studies found that over the long term, the stock prices are more correlated to earnings than free cash flow. The default discount rate is 12 percent. GuruFocus also calculates the margin of safety here, which is calculated as:

$$MOS = (\text{Intrinsic Value} - \text{Price})/\text{Value}$$

You can get the current intrinsic values and the margin of safety of any stock traded worldwide with the discounted cash flow model on GuruFocus.com. The link for Wal-Mart is: http://www.gurufocus.com/dcf/WMT.

A more complex three-stage DCF model can also be set up in a similar way. But it is unnecessary as the calculation itself is an estimate and more assumptions will not give better results.

It's helpful to have the intrinsic value and the margin of safety for the stocks you are interested in, but investors need to be aware of the limitations of the DCF model. First, the DCF model is attempting to predict the future performance of the business. Therefore, the business needs to be predictable. The companies that have steadier growth are more predictable than those with fluctuating earnings. These companies are usually ranked highly with GuruFocus's Business Predictability Rank. The calculation results for those companies are more reliable. The DCF model is not applicable to the companies that have large fluctuations with business performance. The model also does not apply to situations such as asset plays, turnarounds, or cyclicals.

For the companies that have predictable earnings, the assumptions on the calculation parameters can drastically affect the results. The parameters need to be carefully chosen to reflect the real performances of the companies. Next, I discuss the impact of each parameter on the calculation of intrinsic value and how they should be selected in the calculation.

Growth Rates

In GuruFocus's DCF calculator, we assume that in the next ten years a company will grow as fast as it did in the previous ten years. But this will most likely overestimate the growth of the company, especially if the company was growing quickly. Applying a 20 percent growth rate cap reduces overestimation. For example, Priceline averaged 40 percent per year in EPS growth over the past ten years. But for the past five years, the growth rate slowed to about 25 percent. It seems reasonable to assume that it will grow at about 20 percent per year in the next ten years.

For the terminal growth stage, the growth rate of 4 percent per year is probably too low for companies like Priceline. This may underestimate its intrinsic value; 4 percent per year is slightly higher than the long-term inflation rate.

Table 5.1 Dependence of Value on the Growth Rate

Growth Rate	Growth Value	Terminal Value	Total Value
10%	7.9	3.8	11.7
11%	8.3	4.2	12.5
12%	8.7	4.6	13.3
13%	9.1	5.0	14.1
14%	9.5	5.5	15.0
15%	10.0	6.0	16.0
16%	10.5	6.5	17.0
17%	11.0	7.1	18.1
18%	11.6	7.8	19.3
19%	12.1	8.4	20.6
20%	12.7	9.2	21.9
21%	13.4	10.0	23.3
22%	14.0	10.8	24.9
23%	14.7	11.7	26.5
24%	15.5	12.7	28.2
25%	16.3	13.8	30.1

The effect of the growth rate on the value of the business is illustrated in Table 5.1. We assume that the company is earning $1 per share now. Its terminal growth rate is 4 percent. The discount rate is 15 percent. The duration of both the growth period and terminal period is 10. At different growth rates, as reflected in the first column of the table, the value is displayed in the last column.

Obviously, at a higher growth rate, the stock is worth more. If a company grows at 25 percent per year for the first ten years, then grows 4 percent for the next ten, its stock is worth about 30 times its earnings, as we can see from the table. This coincides with Peter Lynch's rule of thumb that a fair P/E ratio for a company is roughly its growth rate. Of course, the fair value calculation result is affected by the discount rate. If the discount rate is 12 percent instead of 15 percent, the values move higher and Lynch's rule of thumb would seem conservative. During Lynch's years at Fidelity, the interest rate was in double digits. The higher discount rate was justified.

Number of Years for Growth and Terminal Stage

The number of years in the growth and terminal stages that are used for calculation can also vastly affect the calculation results. The reasonable assumption for the number of years varies from business to business. If you have teenaged children, like I do, you have surely noticed how they liked Aeropostale T-shirts. The adolescent

T-shirt chain store was unstoppable, growing at 50 percent a year in the early 2000s. Then it hit a wall. Its revenue started to decline in the early 2010s and its stock has since lost more than 99 percent. If we use the DCF model to calculate its intrinsic value in the early 2000s, it would be too generous to assume that it has 20 years of life remaining.

Heard of "live fast, die young"? This saying seems also applicable to the life of businesses. Yet the opposite is also true!

Just as Buffett said, for a business that operates in a fast-changing industry, either no action, or acting too slowly, or acting incorrectly can cost it its life. The businesses that have a long life expectancy are the ones that can sell the same products and services 5, 10, or 20 years from the present. The required change in the business is minimal, and that provides the opportunity to keep improving in making and selling its products while building a network effect, brand recognition, taste habits, and addictions.

Consider Coca-Cola. For more than 100 years, the company has been selling essentially the same soft drink it introduced in the late nineteenth century. The assumption of ten years in the growth stage and another ten in the terminal stage would drastically underestimate the intrinsic value of the company. Curiously, in 1985, almost a century after its debut, Coca-Cola tried to make changes to its product and invented a new formula called "New Coke." But then it found that Coke drinkers preferred the "good old days" and were opposed to the new taste. The company gave in and returned to the old formula. With this lesson behind it, Coca-Cola will probably stay with the same formula for at least another century.

The number of years used in the calculation is how the economic moat is reflected on the intrinsic value of a business. With a wide economic moat, a company can protect its territory and maintain its profitability for the long haul. The number of years used in the calculation needs to be greater.

Another example is See's Candy. For all the future cash flow the company would generate, Buffett paid $25 million in 1972. Table 5.2 uses the real earnings numbers for See's Candy's from 1972 to 1999,[3] except for the years 1973 to 1975, when Berkshire didn't disclose the earnings numbers. Instead, I assumed linear growth from 1972 to 1976. All the earnings after 1972 are discounted to the year of the purchase, 1972, with the discount rate of 25 percent a year. The last column shows the cumulative discounted earnings of See's from 1972 to the year calculated.

Table 5.2   See's Candy Earnings and Discounted Earnings

Year	Pre-tax Earnings ($M)	Discounted Earnings ($)	Cumulative Earnings ($M)
1972	4.2	4.2	4.2
1973	6.0	4.8	9.0
1974	7.8	5.0	14.0
1975	9.5	4.9	18.9
1976	11.0	4.5	23.4
1977	12.8	4.2	27.6
1978	12.5	3.3	30.8
1979	12.8	2.7	33.5
1980	15.0	2.5	36.0
1981	21.9	2.9	39.0
1982	23.9	2.6	41.5
1983	27.4	2.4	43.9
1984	26.6	1.8	45.7
1985	29.0	1.6	47.3
1986	30.4	1.3	48.7
1987	31.7	1.1	49.8
1988	32.5	0.9	50.7
1989	34.2	0.8	51.5
1990	39.6	0.7	52.2
1991	42.4	0.6	52.8
1992	42.4	0.5	53.3
1993	41.2	0.4	53.7
1994	47.5	0.4	54.0
1995	50.2	0.3	54.3
1996	51.9	0.2	54.5
1997	59.0	0.2	54.8
1998	62.0	0.2	55.0
1999	74.0	0.2	55.1

The reason I used a steep 25 percent discount rate is that Buffett was concurrently growing the book value of Berkshire Hathaway at 25 percent a year. Therefore, by 1999, which is the last year that Berkshire reported See's revenue and earnings separately, See's had generated $55 million of pretax earnings in 1972 dollars. If I used a more generous 15 percent discount rate, for Buffett the earnings would be worth $114 million in 1972 dollars. If the discount rate is 12 percent, the cash flow is worth $154 million in 1972 dollars. After paying tax, it is still worth around $100 million. Thus, the $25 million Buffett paid for See's Candy in 1972, which he thought was expensive, was really less than 70 cents on the dollar after the tax payment. It was a bargain, considering the quality of See's business.

Nevertheless, See's life didn't stop in 1999. Just ask the Berkshire shareholders, who stood in long lines to buy the candies during shareholder meetings. To be honest, I find See's chocolates too sweet; I like the nuts and chews better. And those candies are expensive. I wouldn't buy them if I weren't a Berkshire shareholder. Yet See's continues to prosper. In the 15 years from 2000 through 2014, it generated more than $1 billion in pretax earnings for Berkshire Hathaway.[4] The earnings are worth more than $500 million if discounted to year-2000 dollars with a discount rate of 12 percent. Buffett could still sell See's for $500 million in 2000, after generating all the cash flow and originally paying only $25 million. See's life didn't stop in 2014, either. Cash continues to flood in.

I have emphasized the application of the DCF model to Coca-Cola and See's Candy. The point is that the life expectancy of the business is a vital factor when considering buying a company. The companies that have the luxury of changing slowly can stay in business longer and are more valuable to their shareholders.

Is this why the turtle lives so long? I wonder, between the rabbit and the turtle, which one covers more distance during its lifetime.

The effect of the number of terminal years on the intrinsic value is reflected in the table below. Again, we assume that the company is earning $1 now. The discount rate is 12 percent. The growth stage lasted ten years and the growth rate was 12 percent. The terminal growth rate was 4 percent.

# of Terminal Years	Growth Value	Terminal Value	Total Value
10	10.0	6.8	16.8
15	10.0	8.7	18.7
20	10.0	10.0	20.0

We can see that if we increase the number of terminal year growth from 10 to 20, the value of the stock is increased by about 20 percent. Further increase in the number of terminal years will not increase the value by much because of the discount, but a business with a longer life is definitely more valuable.

Discount Rate

I mentioned the effect of the discount rate briefly in the See's Candy calculation. Table 5.3 lists the discounted values for the $859 million

Table 5.3   See's Candy Pretax Earnings as Discounted
to the Year 1972 at Different Discount Rates

Discount Rate	Earnings Discounted to Year 1972 ($million)
25%	55.1
23%	62.1
20%	75.8
17%	95.6
15%	114
12%	153
10%	192

pretax earnings that See's Candy earned from 1972 through 1999 at different discount rates if discounted to the year 1972, when Buffett bought See's. Clearly, the discount rate can also wildly affect the intrinsic value calculation.

So, what is a reasonable discount rate that an investor should use in the calculation of the intrinsic value of a stock? Academically, one should use the weighted average cost of capital (WACC) for the discount rate. But the reasonable discount rate is the rate of return you can achieve if you invest the money somewhere else. If you plan to invest in stocks, the discount rate should be the expected rate of return from a passive investment such as an index fund or ETF. That is why we used a 25 percent discount rate in the calculation for See's Candy—it is the rate of return Buffett was achieving with the book value of Berkshire Hathaway at the time. He could have put that $25 million somewhere else to achieve that kind of return.

If you also consider other options such as bonds, real estate, and so forth, the discount rate should be the rate of return you can expect from those investments plus a risk premium for investing in stocks. For instance, if you can get a risk-free return of 3 percent from a savings account, you should at least use a discount rate of 9 percent, with the additional 6 percent as the equity risk premium.

Therefore, the reasonable discount rate is highly dependent on the rate of return you can achieve from alternative investment options. In the current zero-interest environment, the possible returns from everything from bonds to real estate have declined. The discount rate should be reduced, too. Therefore, the values of stocks have increased. Stocks are traded at high valuations relative to historical levels, but this is probably justified by the current historically low interest rate.

For the example discussed in the previous section, the effect of the discount rate is illustrated in the table below. Both the growth and terminal stages lasted ten years and the growth rate was 12 percent. The terminal growth rate was 4 percent.

Discount Rate	Growth Value	Terminal Value	Total Value
18%	7.59	3.16	10.75
16%	8.29	4.05	12.34
14%	9.08	5.23	14.31
12%	10	6.8	16.8
10%	11.06	8.91	19.97

This is the effect of the interest rate on the discount rate. Buffett calls the interest rate gravity. When the gravity is lower, everything flies higher.

Excess Cash

When Buffett bought See's Candy, the price he paid was actually $35 million instead of $25 million. But See's had $10 million in cash that it did not need in its operations. Buffett did not count that cash into his cost. In estimating the intrinsic value of businesses, any excess cash should be added to the discounted earnings. These days, companies like Microsoft and Apple have a tremendous amount of cash that they don't need for their operations. This cash should be added to the total of future earnings to get a more accurate valuation.

GuruFocus's fair-value calculator has an item called "Tangible Book Value." You can add portions or all of that to the calculation to compensate for the excess cash the company may have.

Earnings vs. FCF

If you look at the intrinsic value equation:

$$\text{Intrinsic Value} = E(0)x(1-x^n)/(1-x) + E(0)x^n y(1-y^m)/(1-y)$$

other than the growth rate and discount rate, intrinsic value is proportional to $E(0)$, which is the earnings for the past year. I haven't distinguished between earnings and free cash flow. The formula applies

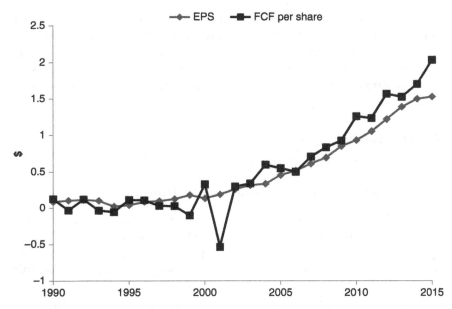

Figure 5.1   CHD EPS vs. FCF

to both. Just replace $E(0)$ with the earnings per share or free cash flow per share, whichever is preferred.

In GuruFocus's DCF calculator, we use earnings instead of free cash flow because our study found that historically the stock performance was more correlated to the earnings than to free cash flow. This finding was a little surprising because free cash flow is the real cash a business generates from its operations. But the free cash in any given year can be affected by the company's spending on property, plant, and equipment (PPE). For a company that is in steady operation, where the DCF model is applicable, the effect of the more random capital spending is smoothed out in earnings through the estimates of depreciation, depletion, and amortization (DDA).

An example is a company called Church & Dwight, which produces Arm & Hammer baking soda and Trojan condoms. Its EPS has been rising steadily, but its free cash flow is doing anything but. In some years, its free cash flow was negative because the company spent more cash on PPE those years. (See Figure 5.1.) Similar behavior was observed with Wal-Mart, which also has steady operations and earnings but fluctuating free cash flow.

In deciding which parameter to use for $E(0)$, be aware of the impact of the onetime effect. Earnings can be distorted by a onetime boost from selling businesses or a tax rebate, or a onetime impairment from write-downs of inventories or other assets. With free cash flow, it may be even more random, as management's decision on spending in the year can have a major impact. The normalized earnings over several years is a better number. GuruFocus uses earnings without nonrecurring items in the past 12 months as the default.

Margin of Safety

The margin of safety is defined as:

$$MOS = (Intrinsic\ Value - Price)/Intrinsic\ Value$$

It is the difference between the intrinsic value and the price that investors are willing to pay relative to the intrinsic value.

A common question is how much margin of safety is enough for one to buy a stock. The answer is, not enough. The more it is, the better.

Although we have beautiful formulae that seem able to calculate the intrinsic value to any accuracy we want, in reality it is only as accurate as the parameters we input for discount rate, the growth rate, the lifetime of the business, and so on. They are affected by factors such as the long-term economic characteristics of the business, the management, and external issues such as future tax rate and inflation, among others. All are about the future, and they come with much uncertainty. The required margin of safety is dependent on the degree of confidence you have regarding these factors.

Furthermore, the intrinsic value of a company is never a fixed number. It changes all the time with the progress of business. A combination of good economic characteristics and capable management can grow the intrinsic value faster, whereas a business with poor economic characteristics can destroy value quickly. To verify this, consider how Buffett has grown the intrinsic value of Berkshire Hathaway while the business values of Sears, JC Penney, BlackBerry, and many other companies have eroded.

I have seen investors put too much belief in DCF calculations. Sometimes we receive questions from GuruFocus users such as why their calculation of the intrinsic value gets $60.01 per share while GuruFocus's DCF calculator gives $59.99 per share. With so many uncertainties in the calculation of intrinsic value, any result is simply an estimate, and the error is much higher than two cents on

60 dollars. The point of the calculation is to give investors a rough idea of where the intrinsic value lies. Remember what John Keynes said: "It is better to be roughly right than precisely wrong."

I have also seen investors dismiss the DCF model completely. To its credit, DCF does give a quite reasonable valuation to the companies that have relatively consistent performance. We can see it from the recent acquisition decisions of Buffett. Berkshire Hathaway acquired BNSF Railway in 2010 for $100 per share, at the time the GuruFocus DCF model assigned an intrinsic value of $91. In 2012 Berkshire acquired Lubrizol Corp. for $135 per share while DCF calculated the value as $114 per share. In 2016 Berkshire acquired Precision Castparts Corp. at $250 per share, and DCF estimates that it was worth $249 per share.

Given the uncertainties with the DCF model, the higher margin of safety is obviously better. The stocks that can be purchased at higher discounts relative to their intrinsic values deliver higher returns to investors. The outperformance comes from the closure of the difference between the intrinsic values and the prices. We may also get higher returns from the deeper discounted price if we get the intrinsic value correct.

Of course, the market doesn't very often sell the stocks we want to buy at the prices we want to pay. As investors, we need to set ourselves an investment hurdle, as Donald Yacktman does with his investing. This hurdle can be the minimum difference between the price we want to pay and the value we will get. This hurdle is the margin of safety.

Reverse DCF

The reverse DCF valuation method is, as its name suggests, the reverse of the DCF model. Instead of assigning an intrinsic value to a business, the reverse DCF tries to see how much future growth is required to justify the current stock price.

The default input parameters of GuruFocus's reverse DCF calculator are:

- Earnings per share: the EPS from the past 12 months (Again, we use earnings instead of free cash flow.)
- The years of growth at the growth stage and the terminal stage: 10

- Terminal growth rate: 4%
- Discount rate: 12%

These parameters are the same as in GuruFocus's DCF calculation. All are adjustable, and adjusting any of them will trigger recalculation.

After you determine the expected growth rate, compare it with the past growth rates and ask yourself if the growth rate is possible with this company. If the calculated growth rate is higher than the past growth rates, the stock price might be ahead of itself. If the calculated growth rate is lower than the past growth rates, the stock might be undervalued.

Similar to the DCF calculation, reverse DCF applies only to the companies that have been profitable and have predictable revenue and earnings growth. Interestingly, when we released GuruFocus's reverse DCF Calculator in March 2013, someone asked why he got an infinite growth rate for Amazon.com. Well, in March 2013, we used Amazon's 2012 annual earnings per share as the default input for earnings, which was negative nine cents. For a company with negative earnings, the DCF model is not applicable and reverse DCF will tell you that no growth rate can justify the current price of the company.

In the case of Apple, the company has grown its revenue by 34 percent per year and its earnings by 47 percent per year over the ten years from 2006 to 2016. Assuming it will grow 20 percent per year over the next ten years, the DCF calculator thinks the stock is worth $243 per share. This is much higher than the current price of $108 per share and gives us a margin of safety of 56 percent. Now, if we switch to reverse DCF, it tells us that at the current price of $108 per share, the company will need to grow its earnings by 7.6 percent per year over the next ten years to justify its current price. Will Apple be able to grow at 7.6 percent per year over the next decade? The company's growth has slowed dramatically over the past 12 months. Will it restore its previous growth? This is the $64,000 Question when it comes to using the reverse DCF calculator.

Fair P/E Ratio

Though Benjamin Graham and Buffett talked extensively about *intrinsic value*, Peter Lynch rarely used the term. He prefers to measure stock valuations with P/E ratio. A growth stock has a fair

P/E ratio; it is where the stock should be traded to justify its earnings and earnings growth.

The fair P/E ratio and the intrinsic value calculation are in fact talking about the same thing. If you look at the intrinsic value equation:

$$\text{Intrinsic Value} = E(0)\,x(1-x^n)/(1-x) + E(0)\,x^n y(1-y^m)/(1-y)$$

the equation for fair P/E should be:

$$\text{Fair P/E} = \text{Intrinsic Value}/E(0)$$
$$= x(1-x^n)/(1-x) + x^n y(1-y^m)/(1-y)$$

Therefore, the fair P/E is dependent on the future growth of the company and the discount rate, just as with intrinsic value. As I mentioned before, if we assume the discount rate is 15 percent, and ten years for both the growth and the terminal stages, and the growth rate is 4 percent, the fair P/E we get is close to the growth rate in percentages. This is Lynch's rule of thumb: that the fair P/E for a growth company is about the same as its earnings growth rate.[5] If the discount rate gets lower, the fair P/E gets higher. This is the situation we are currently in. The interest rate has come to a historical low, which lowers the expected return of all assets and lifts their valuations.

Growth of Value

As I said before, a company's intrinsic value is never a fixed number. It changes as the business evolves. For a business that continues to grow its earnings power while maintaining its competitive advantage, its intrinsic value grows higher.

For example, when Buffett bought See's Candy in 1972, its intrinsic value was really $55.1 million, which is the total of the discounted earnings of the company for the 27 years from 1972 through 1999 at a 25 percent discount rate. When 1999 came, See's was in a position similar to that in 1972. Instead of being "terminated" as predicted in the DCF model, the company seemed to have no problem repeating what it did in the past 27 years, except it was now selling much more candy and at much higher prices. The company was therefore worth far more. At the same discount rate of 25 percent, the company was now worth 18 times what it was in 1972 because it was selling more than 18 times the candies in a dollar amount, and seemed like it would have no problem selling candies for another 27 years. Seventeen years have passed since 1999 and it appears that See's will continue to sell candies—and the business is worth even more. This is the growth of intrinsic value.

Of course, while See's continued to sell more candies for a greater profit and grew its business values, some companies destroyed their values and were indeed terminated. Remember RadioShack, Blockbuster, and Circuit City?

The myth persists that value investors don't value growth enough. The financial market divides investors into different categories: value, growth, momentum, and so on. Actually, value investors love growth. It is true that we love to buy dollar bills for 50 cents; we love it even more if we can pay 50 cents for the dollar bill that is growing. This kind of growth is found in the good companies this book urges readers to buy.

Of course, we don't want to overpay for that growth or for the growth that is not proven. That is probably the difference between value investors and others. Value investors seek to "buy and hold" and grow with the business or "buy low" when a business is undervalued and "sell high" if it becomes overvalued; growth investors look for "emerging" growth companies that have the potential to achieve high earnings growth but have not necessarily established a history of earnings growth; momentum investors try to "buy high and sell higher." Paying $2 for something and hoping to sell it for $3 to someone else is not investing. It is speculating.

We also don't want to pay for the growth that is funded by ever more capital infusion and that loses ever more money as it grows. Incomprehensible as it seems, this is happening in the current market. Many companies become "unicorns," which are supposed to be rare but are no longer. They are valued at tens of billions of dollars as they lose more money to "grow." They spend heavily, bribing customers and hoping that competitors' pockets aren't as deep as theirs. It is a race to the bottom and is not the kind of growth we want to pay for.

I am reminded of a story about the energy secretary during Jimmy Carter's presidency, James Schlesinger.[6] Schlesinger had a Harvard PhD in economics and at one time taught the subject at the University of Virginia. Two of his students were so influenced by him regarding capitalism that upon graduation they went into business.

As the story goes, they were buying up firewood in the Virginia farm country and trucking it to the District of Columbia, where firewood was in high demand. As their business boomed, they found themselves working feverishly, nights and weekends, to meet demand. Thus, they were shocked when their bank reported that their working capital had been depleted and their truck repossessed. It turned out that they paid $60 per cord for the wood and then sold at $55 per cord. They went anxiously to professor Schlesinger and asked where they had gone wrong. Dr. Schlesinger puffed on his signature pipe a long moment before replying, "You should have bought a bigger truck."

A different version of the story was also told by Howard Marks in one of his recent memos.[7] The point is that if a business is selling its products and services at below its cost, the more it grows, the more money it loses. It is not a field in which we want to play.

"All intelligent investing is value investing," as Charlie Munger said.[8]

How Can a Good Company Be Sold at a Low Price?

If a company's business is strong, wouldn't the stock market recognize this and give it a higher valuation? This is a valid question. Good companies are rarely sold cheap because the market does recognize their value most of the time, especially when things are peaceful. But there are so many players in the market—the buy side, the sell side, short sellers, long-term investors, day traders, stock brokers, the media, and the manipulators. They all exist for the same purpose: to make money. But they achieve this purpose in different ways. That's why a company's stock price can fluctuate more than 50 percent in a rather short period while its value barely changes. This gives opportunities to those who are prepared.

Then there are the not-so-peaceful times, which present additional opportunities for long-term investors. These turbulent periods can be divided into three types. The first type is a broad market panic. This usually happens when the economy is in recession and the market has collapsed. Investors have seen deep losses and think that the market will go down forever. So, they give up and sell everything regardless of its quality. Even the best companies are traded at bargain prices during this time. This happened twice in the past 16 years, during the recessions of 2001 and 2008. Each lasted quite a while, and investors had many opportunities to pick up good companies. This is the easiest time to buy great companies at good prices.

The second type is industry-wide distress although the broad market is relatively peaceful. Certain industries are out of favor and the stocks in that industry are traded at lower valuations than the broad market and their historical average. There are opportunities in this industry during such a time. This happened during the market bubble in the late 1990s, when many old-economy stocks were traded at distressed levels and they then outperformed tremendously after the tech bubble burst in the early 2000s. In the past year, energy stocks have been beaten down and have traded at far below their average valuations over the past decade.

The third type is when the broad market is peaceful and no broad opportunities exist in the industries in which you want to invest. This is a harder time to invest, but spots of opportunity may appear from time to time, caused by market manipulators or by influential investment firms. Remember the stock of Fairfax Financial? Short attacks erased 50 percent of its market value while the broad market was going up. Insurance software provider EBIX's stock lost more than 60 percent in less than a year when in 2012 short sellers published articles on popular financial websites to attack it. And steady business operator Church & Dwight saw its stock drop 5 percent when Goldman Sachs downgraded it in January 2016.

Then there are the times when the market panics for other reasons. Lauren Templeton, who is the great-grandniece of Sir John Templeton, compiled a list of these a few years ago:[9]

- Attack on Pearl Harbor (1941)
- Korean War (1950)
- President Eisenhower's heart attack (1955)
- Blue Monday (1962)
- Cuban missile crisis (1962)
- President Kennedy assassination (1963)
- Black Monday 1987 crash
- United Airlines LBO failure (1989)
- Persian Gulf War (1990)
- Tequila crisis (1994)
- Asian financial crisis (1997–98)
- September 11 (2001)
- Financial crisis 2008–2009
- European debt crisis (2010–2015)

I can add recent events, such as:

- U.S. government debt-ceiling crisis (2011)
- Ebola outbreak (2014)
- Brexit referendum (2016)

Thankfully, during the Ebola outbreak in 2014, only 11 people in the United States contracted the disease, and 9 of them were exposed outside the country. The market panicked anyway and quickly lost 10 percent.

How to be ready to react to these events? "Preparation, preparation, preparation," just as Lauren Templeton said.

And from Charlie Munger: "Opportunity meeting the prepared mind; that's the game. Opportunity doesn't come often, so seize it when it comes." So, act quickly when the time comes!

Of course, it is not easy to buy stocks when everyone else is selling, or when some powerful brokerage house is downgrading the stock. But this is the time to make a difference in your performance over that of others. Understand the nature of the business you want to buy and know the price you want to pay. Build enough confidence in your research and have enough conviction to act when opportunities arise. Independent thinking is the basic requirement for an investor to succeed, and independent thinking is built on knowledge and hard work.

If you haven't built the necessary confidence, stay away from the stock. If you have conducted solid research and have built a watch list for the stocks you want to buy, and know the price you want to pay, the opportunities will come.

Wouldn't It Be Even Better to Buy Good Companies at Lower Prices?

It is certainly better if we can buy good companies at low prices. But, most times you don't get to do this. In his early years running Berkshire Hathaway, Buffett was looking to buy "wonderful companies at very attractive prices." As Berkshire grew larger and Buffett had far more money to invest, he gradually changed it to: "wonderful companies at attractive prices." Later he again adjusted it to: "wonderful companies at fair prices." Two factors changed his mindset. One is that his portfolio was getting so large, his investment universe had shrunk to only big companies.[10] The other is market conditions. In an expensive market, it is simply impossible to find good companies at attractive prices.

Most of us don't have the problem of having too much money like Buffett. We just need to be patient and wait for opportunities. But what is the fair price to pay? A fair price is when you can still get above-market-average returns over the long term through the investment. With a fair price, you don't get additional returns from the closure of the gap between the price and the intrinsic value. Your returns are solely from the growth of the intrinsic value of the company. With the good company you are buying, the company is able to grow its value faster than the market average and you as a shareholder are rewarded.

Still, buying good companies at fair prices is far better than buying fair companies at good prices. You don't want to overpay, even for a good company. Remember the examples of Wal-Mart and Coca-Cola? If you pay too much, the closure of the price and intrinsic value works against you even when the company is growing its value faster than the market average.

Summary

I have used some formulas in this chapter to illustrate the DCF model and fair P/E. That makes stock valuation look like rocket science. But it is not. The formula itself is simple and the calculator is readily available online. The key is to choose which parameters to use, and that requires a full understanding of the underlying business. Without carefully choosing the parameters, there is no point in performing a DCF calculation.

Furthermore, there are many ways to evaluate a business. DCF calculation is just one, and it is only applicable to a very small subset of companies that have predictable revenue and earnings. The point of DCF or any other calculation is to give you a rough idea of where the right price rests for the stock. Always leave yourself a margin of safety.

At times, you will not be able to find any stocks of the good companies worth buying. It is time, then, to get prepared and wait for the opportunities to be presented by the market. And don't forget, before doing any calculation, investors should always look at the company's business and answer one question: Is this the good company we want to buy?

Buy only good companies and buy them at reasonable prices.

C H A P T E R

Buy Good Companies: The Checklist

"If the path be beautiful, let us not ask where it leads."
—Anatole France

I have spent three chapters examining good companies and fair prices. The idea is simple, but the details are complex. I want now to summarize the idea and process in a simple checklist.

Every investor should create his or her own investing checklist, no matter how he or she chooses to invest. As discussed extensively in his bestselling book, *The Checklist Manifesto: How to Get Things Right*,[1] Atul Gawande wrote that checklists have been widely used in the medical and aviation industries because they simplify complex procedures and help doctors and pilots maintain their composure and discipline.

When US Airways Flight 1549 from LaGuardia Airport to Charlotte hit a large flock of birds and lost both of its engines, the first thing pilot Sully Sullenberger and his crew did was get out their checklists, according to Sullenberger's memoir, *Highest Duty: My Search for What Really Matters*.[2] Humans being human, mistakes will inevitably occur. Checklist usage catches the errors, sets discipline and process, and helps avoid potential losses.

Hedge fund manager Mohnish Pabrai likens buying a stock to the takeoff of an airplane. Many successful investors have their own checklists to guide their investment processes, although they might not explicitly call them such. For example, Walter Schloss, the notable disciple of Benjamin Graham, averaged 15.3 percent compound return over the course of four and a half decades, versus 10 percent for the S&P 500, and followed his own 16 rules of investing, which cover valuation, discipline, conviction, and leverage.[3] Philip Fisher, the father of growth investing, always asks himself 15 questions about the company he is interested in buying. He detailed these 15 questions in his book, *Common Stocks and Uncommon Profits*, and they cover the areas of market potential, management, the effectiveness of research and development, profit margin, labor relations, and share buybacks.[4] Peter Lynch has a long list of questions he asks about each company, which can be different depending on the specific company situation.[5]

Checklist for Buying Good Companies at Reasonable Prices

Here, I summarize the questions we will ask for investing in good companies at fair prices, which have been examined in detail in previous chapters.

1. Do I understand the business?
2. What is the economic moat that protects the company so it can sell the same or a similar product five or ten years from today?
3. Is this a fast-changing industry?
4. Does the company have a diversified customer base?
5. Is this an asset-light business?
6. Is it a cyclical business?
7. Does the company still have room to grow?
8. Has the company been consistently profitable over the past ten years, through good times and bad?
9. Does the company have a stable double-digit operating margin?
10. Does the company have a higher margin than competitors?
11. Does the company have a return on investment capital of 15 percent or higher over the past decade?
12. Has the company been consistently growing its revenue and earnings at double digits?
13. Does the company have a strong balance sheet?
14. Do company executives own decent shares of stock of the company?
15. How are the executives paid compared with other similarly sized companies?

16. Are insiders buying?
17. Is the stock valuation reasonable as measured by intrinsic value, or P/E ratio?
18. How is the current valuation relative to historical range?
19. How did the company's stock price fare during the previous recessions?
20. How much confidence do I have in my research?

For the first 19 questions, we focus on the areas of business nature (questions 1–7), performance (questions 8–12), financial strength (question 13), management (questions 14–16), and valuation (questions 17–19).

The final question centers on how you feel about your research. Though it is not directly related to the company, your own analysis is a vital consideration. It determines your action once the stock suddenly drops 50 percent after you buy. That same 50 percent drop can trigger opposing actions depending on your level of confidence. If you are assured in your research, the 50 percent drop in price is a great opportunity to buy more of the stock at half the price. If you don't have confidence, you will likely be scared into selling at a 50 percent loss.

Trust me, it will happen after you buy the stock; and, paradoxically, it happens only after you buy. So, get prepared!

The Warning Signs

When you buy a house, you not only want to make sure that it meets your checklist of requirements on location, size, number of bedrooms and baths, and so on; you also want to make sure it doesn't have any hidden problems with the foundation, electrical system, AC, or plumbing—which is why you perform a home inspection. Therefore, in addition to the checklist that screens the stocks that meet our requirements, we also want to screen for things we don't want. GuruFocus developed a feature called Warning Signs, which undertakes a thorough inspection on the financial health and performance of companies. These warning signs are highlighted for each company. The purpose of Warning Signs is to advise you of red flags in certain areas of the company that you may have overlooked. These warning signs do not necessarily mean you should avoid buying the stock, but you should be aware of and accept them before you invest.

The Warning Signs checkup covers these areas:

- *Financial strength*

Financial strength of the company is ranked according to its debt burden as measured by interest coverage, debt-to-revenue ratio, and Altman Z-Score, and is ranked from one to ten. A rating of eight or above reflects strong financial strength. More on Altman Z-Score later in the list.

The distribution of the financial strength of U.S. companies is represented in Figure 6.1. Not surprisingly, most of the companies have an average financial strength. The companies that have a financial strength rating of seven or higher are considered financially strong.

If a company has a financial strength of four or less, investors need to watch out for an associated bankruptcy risk. A warning sign is triggered.

- *Profitability rank*

A company's profitability is ranked based on its operating margin, Piotroski F-Score, the trend of the operating margin, and the consistency of the profitability. More on Piotroski F-Score later in this list.

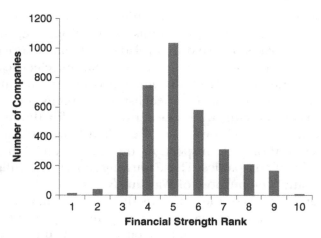

Figure 6.1   Financial Strength Distribution

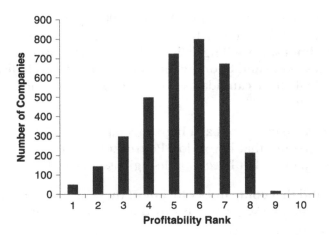

Figure 6.2   Profitability Distribution

The distribution of the profitability ranking of U.S. companies is depicted in Figure 6.2. A company with the profitability ranking of four or less gets a warning on profitability.

- *Revenue, earnings growth rate of ten-year, five-year, three-year, and one-year periods*

This checks if the revenue or profit of the company is declining in any given period. If it is, a warning sign is triggered.

- *Operating losses*

This checks if the company has experienced operating loss over the past ten years. If so, a warning sign is triggered.

- *Gross margin growth, operating margin growth*

This checks if the gross margin and/or the operating margin of the company are declining. If any of the margins are, a warning sign is triggered.

- *Asset growth faster than revenue growth*

If a company's asset growth grows faster than its revenue growth, it means the company is becoming less efficient, especially if its asset growth is caused by borrowing. In May 2008, James Montier, fund manager at GMO, couldn't find opportunities to invest. He wrote an article about short selling called "Mind Matters: Joining the Dark Side: Pirates, Spies and Short Sellers" and in his research discovered that the ideal short candidates are the companies that have these three characteristics:[6]

1. Stocks that are sold at a high P/S ratio
2. Companies that have a low Piotroski F-Score
3. Companies that have double-digit asset growth

He found that companies with any of these characteristics under-performed the market, which is why this is a warning sign.

- *Days sales outstanding*

Days sales outstanding measures how quickly the company can get paid after delivering its products. It is a financial ratio that illustrates how well a company's accounts receivable are being managed. Here we compare the average of days sales outstanding over the past 12 months with the average of the past five years. If it is getting longer, a warning sign is triggered. A longer days sales outstanding means that it takes more time for the company to get paid after a sale has been made, or it is selling its products on credit.

- *Days sales of inventory*

Days sales of inventory measures how quickly the company turns its inventory into sales. If this indicator is getting longer, it means that the company is having difficulty selling. We compare the average days sales of inventory of the past 12 months with the average of the past five years. If it is getting longer, a warning sign is triggered.

It is typical for a retailer to increase its inventory before the holiday season because it usually does more sales during this time than any other time. Therefore, this parameter needs to be compared with the same period from the previous year.

- *Owner earnings diverged from reported earnings*

Owner earnings is a concept Warren Buffett introduced in his 1986 shareholder letter.[7] It measures the true earnings of the company from its existing operations to its owners. It is an estimated number from the financial statements of the company. If there is a long-term deviation between the owner earnings and reported earnings, a warning sign is triggered.

- *Divergence between net income and free cash flow*

Similar to owner earnings, free cash flow measures the net cash generated by the business. If there is a long-term deviation between the two, a warning sign is triggered.

When a company is in fast expansion, its earnings are usually reinvested into the business, which lowers its free cash flow. It doesn't necessarily mean there is something wrong with the company.

- *Cost of capital higher than the return on invested capital*

I have referenced return on invested capital many times. A company creates real returns only if its return on invested capital is higher than its cost of capital. For the purpose of the warning signs' checklist, however, if the cost of capital is higher than the return on capital, a warning sign is triggered.

- *Issuance of debt*

If the company keeps issuing new debt, it likely means that it cannot generate enough cash to fund its operations. This is certainly a warning sign. With more debt, the company may earn more, but its debt burden gets higher and its balance sheet gets weaker.

- *Issuance of new shares*

Similarly, if a company keeps issuing new shares, it probably means that it cannot generate enough cash to fund its operations and it cannot borrow. This is also a warning sign. With more shares, the shareholders are diluted.

If a company's stock price is at a very high valuation, issuing new shares benefits existing shareholders. In this warning sign, we don't distinguish the prices at which the company issues new shares.

- *Altman Z-Score*

Altman Z-Score was developed by NYU Stern finance professor Edward Altman in 1967.[8] His study found that the score is an accurate forecaster of bankruptcy risk within two years. Therefore, it is also a measurement of a company's financial health, and thus, we use it to rank the financial strength of companies. It is calculated from the company's working capital, retained earnings, market cap, and so on. You can find a detailed example of the calculation and explanation by using this link: http://www.gurufocus.com/term/zscore/WMT/ Altman-Z-Score/Wal-Mart-Stores-Inc.

If the Altman Z-Score is too low, a warning sign is triggered.

- *Piotroski F-Score*

Piotroski F-Score was developed by University of Chicago professor Joseph Piotroski in 2000.[9] It uses nine indicators to measure a company's profitability, the changes in its profitability, leverage, efficiency, its quality of earnings, and so on. It gives a score between zero and nine for each company. The higher the score, the better. If the score is too low, a warning sign is triggered.

A detailed example of F-score calculation can be found here: http://www.gurufocus.com/term/fscore/WMT/Piotroski-F-Score/ Wal-Mart-Stores-Inc.

- *Beneish M-Score*

Beneish M-Score checks the quality of reported earnings and is an indicator that measures if the company manipulates its earnings. It was developed by Indiana University professor Messod Beneish in 1999,[10] and it considers the relationship between accounts receivable, revenue, gross profit, current assets, depreciation, current liabilities, and others to determine the quality of earnings. A higher score indicates that the company might be manipulating its earnings.

You can find a detailed example of Beneish M-Score calculation here: http://www.gurufocus.com/term/mscore/WMT/Beneish-M-Score/Wal-Mart-Stores-Inc.

- *Sloan ratio*

Sloan ratio emerged from the 1996 study by Richard Sloan, a former University of Michigan researcher.[11] He found that if a company's earnings include a significant amount of noncash earnings, its stock underperforms. Sloan ratio is calculated as the ratio of noncash earnings to assets. Therefore, Sloan ratio can be used to measure the quality of earnings. If Sloan ratio is high, a warning sign is triggered.

An example of the Sloan-ratio calculation can be found here: http://www.gurufocus.com/term/sloanratio/WMT/Sloan-Ratio/ Wal-Mart-Stores-Inc.

- *Interest coverage*

I have explained interest coverage in detail. It is defined as the ratio of a company's operating income to the interest payment on its debt. The higher the ratio is, the lower the debt burden is. Therefore, it is also a measure of the financial health of the company. If the interest coverage is low, a warning sign is triggered.

- *Dividend payout ratio*

Dividend payout ratio is the ratio of annual dividend per share to its annual earnings per share. Dividend is the cash distribution of earnings to shareholders. It comes from earnings and must be supported by earnings. If a company's dividend is consistently a large percentage (e.g., 80%) of earnings, it may not be sustainable.

- *Short percentage of float*

This warning sign triggers when the company's shares are heavily shorted. In Chapter 4, I used the example of short attacks on Fairfax Financial, where the stock was manipulated by the short attackers. But many times, short sellers are right. Companies do lie, and short attackers can police their acts. A study by former University of Chicago researcher Owen Lamont in 2003 found that in the three years after the attacks by short sellers between 1977 and 2002, the companies' stocks underperformed by 42 percent on average, even though these companies professed innocence by suggesting they were the subjects of a bear raid or conspiracies, or they alleged that the short sellers were lying.[12] The shorts were mostly right—often it was the companies that were lying and conspiring to defraud investors, not the reverse! The short sellers may know something that others don't.

Of course, this is not always the case. In the example of the Fairfax Financial short attack in the mid-2000s and the high-profile short attack on EBIX and Herbalife in the mid-2010s, the companies were found by government investigators to have committed no wrongdoing. The settlements turned out to be much smaller than the short sellers had advertised and hoped for. In all situations, it is important to understand the short theses of the attackers.

Many of them attacked the companies to manipulate the stock prices for short-term gains, too. In any case, it is a warning sign when the short ratio is high.

- *Dividend yield relative to historical range*

Here we check the current dividend yield relative to its historical range for the periods of ten years, five years, three years, and one year. If the current dividend yield is close to the historical lows, a warning sign is triggered. Usually a lower dividend yield is associated with a higher price.

- *Stock price relative to historical range*

This item checks the current price relative to the historical price range for the periods of ten years, five years, three years, and one year. If the stock price is close to historical highs, a warning sign is triggered.

- *Valuation ratios P/E, P/B, P/S relative to historical range*

This item checks where the valuation ratios price-to-earnings (P/E), price-to-book (P/B), and price-to-sales (P/S) currently stand relative to their historical ranges for the periods of ten years, five years, three years, and one year. Normally, you don't want to buy a stock when it is most expensive relative to where it was traded historically. If any of the valuation ratios are close to historical highs, the warning sign is triggered.

- *Higher forward P/E*

Forward P/E is calculated as the current stock price divided by the next year's earnings as estimated by analysts. If a company's forward P/E is higher than the current P/E, it means that Wall Street analysts expect its earnings to decline. This is a warning sign. There can be big misses from analysts' estimates.

- *Buyback track record*

If a company is buying back its own stock, it is usually considered a positive sign. With this item, we check the track record of the company with its buybacks over the past. If it doesn't have a good track record, the warning sign is triggered. This means that the company is not good at timing its buybacks.

- *All insiders selling and no insiders buying*

If a company's executives and directors are selling its shares heavily, and no insider buys, a warning sign is triggered.

- *Tax rate*

In principle, if a company pays a lower tax rate, it is good for shareholders. But if a company claims good earnings but pays a lower tax rate, investors need to know why. Is this due to a tax haven, poor quality of earnings, or other reasons? This warning sign triggers if the tax rate the company pays is too low.

■■■

We perform a thorough inspection of the company with these questions, just like the annual checkups we undergo at a doctor's office. It is impossible for a company to trigger no warning signs. These warning signs may not stop us from buying the stock, but they should be taken into consideration when we buy.

The checkup questions are based on the company's financial data. Therefore, none of them should replace your work of understanding the business and learning about its products, its customers, its suppliers, its competitors, and the people who work in the company. The warning signs serve as reminders of where you are. They are not meant to substitute for understanding. If we paid attention only to the numbers and signs and ignored the business itself, we would be like the business consultant in this joke:

> A man flying in a hot-air balloon suddenly realizes he's lost. He reduces height and spots a man below. He lowers the balloon and shouts, "Excuse me. Can you tell me where I am?"
>
> The man below says: "Yes. You're in a hot-air balloon, hovering thirty feet above this field."
>
> "You must work in business consulting," says the balloonist.
>
> "I do," replies the man. "How did you know?"
>
> "Well," says the balloonist, "everything you have told me is technically correct, but it's of no use to anyone."
>
> The man below says, "You must work in management."
>
> "I do," replies the balloonist. "But how'd you know?"
>
> "Well," says the man below, "you don't know where you are or where you're going, but you expect me to be able to help. You're in the same position you were before we met, but now it's my fault."

If we gain a solid understanding of the business, these numbers and signs will help us to appreciate where we are and where we are probably going. If business understanding is qualitative and the numbers are quantitative, both are needed to gain the confidence we need for our research.

Positive Signs

In opposition to the warning signs, some signs are positive and indicate that the company is improving its operation or that management is more confident about the company. These signs are complementary to the strong balance sheet, high business returns, and revenue and earnings growth that come with the good companies we want to buy.

- *Profit-margin growth*

Long-term and steady growth in profit margins is a strong indication that the company is doing well. As the company grows its sales, it gets better at what it does and becomes more productive; also, its customer acquisition cost may not grow as fast, which leads to faster profit growth than sales growth, that is, profit-margin growth.

Long-term, steady profit-margin growth can be powerful. For example, AutoZone, the auto parts retailer, was able to grow its gross margin from 48.9 percent in 2005 to above 52 percent in 2015. This increase of gross margin was achieved mainly by lower product acquisition costs and lower shrinkage expenses. Although 3 percent doesn't look like a lot, most of this enhancement is translated into the improvement in operating margins, which increased from 17.08 percent in 2005 to 19.17 percent in 2015. The seemingly small improvement of 6.3 percent in gross margin results in a much higher 12 percent improvement in operating margin. Therefore, during the past ten years, AutoZone's earnings have been growing faster than its sales growth. Its return on invested capital improved from 30 percent in 2005 to 46 percent in 2015. Its stock gained more than 700 percent during this period.

For any business, even if it is at the same level of operation, its operating cost gradually increases because of inflation-induced higher costs of salary, rent, and maintenance. It has to grow its sales at least faster than inflation to be sustainable over the long term.

Two things can lead to profit-margin growth. I want to use the example of a retail chain to explain. For a chain store that grows by opening more stores, its cost on inventory management, marketing, and administration does not grow as fast as the number of its stores. As the company opens more stores, its profit margin increases. This is growth-driven profit-margin growth. If the chain store no longer opens new stores, it can still make more money by selling more at each store. This is productivity-driven profit-margin growth.

The two parts of profit growth can exist at the same time. A company must control cost as it grows. The productivity-driven profit-margin growth is an indication of the competitiveness and pricing power of the business.

- *Share buyback*

Instead of issuing new shares that dilute shareholder value, the company is buying back shares. Usually the buyback is considered as returning value to shareholders. It may drive up the stock prices as the profits are now distributed on a smaller number of shares.

Not all share buybacks are created equal, as pointed out by Buffett. Share buyback is valuable only if the company buys back its shares at below the intrinsic value of the stocks. If a company buys back at above the stock's intrinsic value, it destroys value for the remaining shareholders over the long term. This is why Buffett set a threshold for the share buyback at Berkshire Hathaway, which is 1.2 times the book value of the shares.

We have observed all kinds of behavior with companies' buybacks. Companies like AutoZone, Wal-Mart, and Moody's have been buying back every year since 2000. They buy back their shares without regard for the valuation. Others, like Netflix, sometimes bought back shares, but issued more shares at other times. With the interest rate at all-time lows, as it is currently, some companies issued debt to support the share buyback.

Share buyback inevitably weakens the balance sheet of the company. While enjoying the support of stock prices by share buybacks, investors need to look at long-term effects. In the first half of the 2000s, Washington Mutual, the largest savings and loan bank at the time, spent billions to buy back its shares. When the financial crisis hit in 2008, the company became insolvent and was seized by the government, and shareholders lost all their money. Washington

Mutual would have been in a much better position had it kept the cash on its balance sheet. Sears spent close to $5 billion buying back shares from 2006 to 2013. Now it has to borrow money to support its continuing struggle. Its market cap is less than one-fifth of what it spent on buybacks. The buyback benefited only those who sold out at the time. The remaining shareholders were left holding the bag.

- *Raising dividends*

If a company is raising dividends, it means that the company is confident in its profitability. It is a positive sign. But as with share buybacks, paying dividends weakens the balance sheet of the company. Investors need to think about its effect over the long term.

- *Paying down debt*

Paying down debt is always good for a company to do, although it may reduce return on equity as the company is now less leveraged.

- *Insider buying*

The only reason insiders are buying their own company's shares is because they think they will go up, as Lynch pointed out. Academic studies also found that insiders are mostly long-term value investors. They buy their own company stocks when they think their companies are favorable as long-term investments.[13]

■ ■ ■

The checklist is a useful tool for investors to maintain discipline in their stock picking. The warning signs and positive signs can help investors gain a deeper understanding of the company and build the confidence necessary to direct their future actions.

Lynch once suggested that investors write a note for every stock they research and buy, then compare the company's business performance with these notes over time to see if the original investment thesis still holds.[14] The checklist, warning signs, and positive signs explained in this chapter should also be included in the research notes.

With all these procedures, we hope to reduce errors and failures and avoid the value traps that ensnare many value investors.

Failures, Errors, and Value Traps

"Some things happen for a reason. Others just come with the season."

—Ana Claudia Antunes

I have spent many pages detailing the reasons why we should buy only good companies. With a good company, time is on your side. If you can buy at an attractive price, you will achieve great returns. If you can buy at a fair price, you grow with the company and will still do well. If you pay a high price, over time the growth of the business value will compensate for the initial cost. Although your return will be subpar, you will still be able to someday get your money back.

With a company that is eroding value, the risk you face is the permanent loss of capital. This is why I would rather buy the right company and pay a little more than buy the wrong company on the cheap.

There are many ways to lose money in the stock market. Beginning investors lose money on hot stocks and speculation. Growth investors expect speculative growth to endure and pay too much for it. Value investors are addicted to price bargains and overlook the quality of the underlying business.

The stock market is just weird. Every time someone sells, someone else buys, and they both think they're smart!

The Wrong Companies

You can easily lose a lot of money in the stock market by buying when the market is exciting and optimistic, then selling when it is distressed and in a panic. Or by playing with stock options and futures or by buying on margins—if you do, you can lose money with almost any stock. Even if you are a long-term investor in a relatively peaceful bull market, you can still lose money by buying the wrong companies—ones that are on their way to failing or that may survive but will never reach a point to justify the price you paid.

Next, I summarize the signs that may indicate you are buying a wrong company. These warning signs are different from what I described in the previous chapter. The warning signs that follow are focused on the business behaviors of a company. If you recognize any of these signs related to the company's business operation, you may want to avoid buying at any price.

It Has a Hot Product with a Bright Future

These are usually young companies in hot industries. Their products are typically involved in revolutionary technology that is disruptive and can have enormous impact on society. Many ambitious young entrepreneurs start companies within the field because the technology is promising; it changes people's lives, so investors are excited about its bright prospects and buy into the future of the technology.

As the technology matures, it becomes evident that it did change people's lives. But the field is too crowded. Few companies will become profitable and survive. Those that do can create immense wealth for their investors, whereas most other investors lose money because their companies cannot turn a profit. Many more may never have any meaningful revenue.

Beginning and amateur investors can easily get into this situation, like I did when I started out. I bought into fiber optics because the technology was so promising and suggested the brightest future. The technology did dramatically increase the speed of the Internet and made possible many applications, like video streaming, mobile Internet, and online gaming, but the surfeit of companies just couldn't generate a profit and could never justify their past valuation.

This happens once every few years in new fields, and it occurs more frequently now than in the past due to the acceleration of technology and innovations. In the past century, it was the flight industry, the automobile industry, semiconductors, digital watches, computer hardware, software, the Internet, dot-coms, and fiber optics. For this century, it has so far been solar technology, biotech, social media, electric cars, and so on.

Starting in the mid-2000s, with the support and incentives of governments from the United States to China, solar technology was booming. The technology was promising because it is clean and cannot be depleted, and we seem to be running out of oil and gas. The advance of technology has lowered the cost to more economically viable levels. It is revolutionary. Even Thomas Edison once said: "I'd put my money on the sun and solar energy. What a source of power! I hope we don't have to wait until oil and coal run out before we tackle that."

Hundreds of solar-panel companies popped up worldwide, many of them publicly traded, and it seemed to be a wonderful opportunity for investors to participate in the booming new technology. Investors bid up the stock prices and created new wealth. Shi Zhengrong, the founder of Chinese solar company Suntech Power Holdings, became China's richest person at the time, with a net worth of more than $2 billion as Suntech was traded on the NYSE with a market cap of $12 billion. U.S. solar companies SunEdison, First Solar, and SunPower Corp. were all traded at above $10 billion in market cap.

But the competition is brutal, and it is also global. As with any new technology, new investments poured in, adding more to the competition; the technology then advanced quickly, and the crowded field produced much more capacity than the market can digest. The price of solar panels collapsed. There is no winner. Suntech Power and SunEdison are now bankrupt. First Solar and SunPower both lost more than 80 percent of their market values from 2008. SunPower is still losing money. SolarCity, a relatively new player that lays solar panel on people's roofs and has visionary entrepreneur Elon Musk as its chairman and largest shareholder, cannot make it alone and has merged into another of Musk's companies, Tesla Motors. Tesla has its own problems. It has never made a profit, either, and its losses are mounting. It is also in a similarly hot field that more players are entering. It is now rumored that even Apple is planning to make cars. It feels just like the fiber optics bubble I so painfully experienced.

Don't get me wrong. Solar energy did have a bright future. It still has. It is becoming more cost-effective and its market share has increased. As a former scientist and inventor, I am not against new technology and innovations. New technology and innovations improve people's lives. They just don't make good investments.

It Has a Hot Product that Everyone Is Buying

Remember the days when almost every child wore a pair of Crocs? Or every teenager wore an Aeropostale T-shirt? They were cool and kids loved them. Crocs' sales tripled in 2006 from the year before, then more than doubled in 2007. Aeropostale's sales grew more than 20 percent every year from 2004 through 2009. While the kids' parents bought the shoes and the T-shirts, they bought the stocks, too. Crocs' stocks were traded at a market cap of more than $6 billion. Aeropostale was traded at close to $3 billion.

But those shoes are now ugly, and no one wants to wear a T-shirt with *AERO* emblazoned across the front. Crocs was able to diversify its products into additional areas and is selling more shoes than before. But its stock has lost more than 80 percent and is traded at less than $1 billion in market cap. Aeropostale just cannot get back its cool and has filed for bankruptcy.

It is acceptable to buy the stocks if you love the companies' products, but make sure growth is sustainable and the company is profitable. This is why we select only companies that have been profitable for at least ten years to qualify as a good company. The concept must be proven for at least a full market cycle; we don't want to get caught up in a fad.

It Is at the Peak of the Cycle

The earnings are good and its stock valuation looks low. But it is actually a cyclical business that is at its peak. Cyclicals like automakers, airlines, and durable goods producers have good earnings at the peak of the cycle, which makes their P/E low and the stock attractive. P/S and P/B ratios relative to their historical range are better indicators of where they are with valuation. If the company produces commodities like oil, coal, steel, gold, and so forth, it is also necessary to consider where the prices of the commodities are relative to their historical range. When they are at the high end of the historical range, they are likely to go lower. I will explain more about investing in cyclical companies in Chapter 9.

We have heard a lot of turnaround stories with cyclicals. But usually it is not because the management has special skills, but instead simply because their market comes back. If recession hits again, the management will probably discover that "we succeeded in turning around the business ... just in the wrong direction."

We want to avoid cyclicals, but if you are determined to buy, the best time is when cyclicals are at the bottom of the cycle, when the news is bad, and they may be losing money. Many of them cannot make it through and in turn go bankrupt. Buy those with the solidest financial strength and that are able to make it through the bad times. Also, remember to sell them when things look good and they are again generating large profit. Unlike the consistently profitable companies, cyclicals will again fall into trouble when the industry gets into a down cycle.

It Is Growing Fast

You want the company you buy to grow, but you don't want it to grow too fast. If a company grows too quickly, it may not be able to hire enough qualified employees to maintain quality of products and customer service. This is what happened to Krispy Kreme in the early 2000s and Starbucks in the mid-2000s. Starbucks had to close more than 900 unprofitable locations and focus on its core business.

Furthermore, such companies may need more capital than they can generate to fund the fast growth, causing a cash crunch and forcing them to borrow. If there is any hiccup in the economy or the business itself, they may not be able to service their debt and could face bankruptcy risk.

Tesla is growing fast, with its Model 3 wait time said to be three years. The company is spending heavily to ramp up its manufacturing capacity. In the meantime, as it sells more cars, it loses more money. Tesla's stock has done well for those who bought before 2013, so far. And remember, it just bought SolarCity, which was also a fast grower facing an even worse cash-flow problem. With Tesla's mounting loss and debt, and a merger with a company that was in worse shape, I will stay away from it.

Growing too fast is dangerous. When a company is growing fast, watch its cash.

It Is an Aggressive Serial Acquirer

Companies can also grow through acquisition, which is even more dangerous. I can find far more examples of companies that get into trouble by acquiring others. Driven by ambitious CEOs, many companies grow by acquiring their competitors. They pay a high price for the acquisition and get themselves deep into debt. This was what happened with Canadian drugmaker Valeant. After Michael Pearson became its CEO in 2010, the company went on a shopping spree. Through multiple acquisitions every year, its revenue grew from less than $1 billion in 2009 to more than $10 billion in 2015. For quite a while, Valeant was the hottest stock from the United States to Canada. Investors cheered the growth by driving its stock up more than 20 times. Pearson was considered capable and was the highest-paid CEO in the world. In the meantime, the company's long-term debt ballooned from $380 million to $30 billion. Then its luck ran out and the company found itself under SEC investigation. Its acquisition growth model collapsed and Pearson was ousted. The stock has lost 85 percent from its peak, with Valeant still losing money and the debt bomb ticking.

If a company is too aggressive with acquisition, watch its debt.

Its Business Is Too Competitive

No business is immune to competition, which is why a business must build an economic moat with high quality, low cost, brand recognition, high switching cost through network effect, and so on. Different businesses compete in different ways and at different scales. A restaurant mainly competes with other restaurants in the same area. A technology company's competition can come from anywhere on the globe.

If a company sells commodity products, it cannot differentiate itself through products. It has to compete via prices. The ones with the lowest cost win. Commodity products include oil, gas, agricultural products, airline tickets, and insurance. Over time, many high-tech products become commodities, too. Think TVs and computers. Now even smartphones are becoming commodities.

Retail is an especially tough business because almost everything a store sells can be found somewhere else, and everything it does can be easily imitated by its competitors. Retail stores' competition used to be local, but now is global and online. Those with higher costs cannot survive, and we have seen many closed. Still remember Circuit City, Sport Authority, and K-Mart? Department-store business is among the most competitive; somehow there are always too many of them. In 1977, Warren Buffett lost money on a department store called Vornado Inc. He wrote: "It turned out that the industry was over-stored, and Vornado and the rest of the discounters were getting killed by competition from K-Mart stores."[1] Even K-Mart is long gone, and the industry is just as overstored as it was 40 years ago.

The shift of consumers to online shopping makes the department-store business even worse. We will continue to see the struggle of the likes of JC Penney, Macy's, Sears, and so on. In an industry that competes at such fierce intensity, no one wins.

It Does Everything to Gain Market Share

It is not always good for a business to have more customers. A business needs to be selective with customers and price its products at a level that is competitive but profitable. Attention should be focused on the customers who are loyal and profitable. Trying to gain market share through aggressive pricing puts a business's survivability in danger.

Doing everything to gain market share can be fatal to financial institutions like banks and insurance. The adverse effect usually doesn't show up until several years later, which is why they need a strict underwriting process to qualify customers and price the potential loss properly. It wasn't long ago that banks relaxed their underwriting standards and gave loans to subprime borrowers who would otherwise not qualify. They got into price wars with loans that offered "zero down, zero percent, and zero payment." The financial crisis caused by subprime loans eventually drove the world's financial system to the brink of collapse. The banks that had the most exposure were punished most heavily, too. Many of them are gone and forgotten.

Insurance companies can get into deep trouble if they take on too many customers without pricing the risk properly. In the early 1970s, GEICO almost destroyed itself because it wanted to gain more market share. It charged too little for its car-insurance policies. The company was on the verge of bankruptcy before increasing prices and getting out of the states where it was unprofitable. By doing that, it lost market share but became profitable again. When I bought my first house in 2000, I insured it through an insurer called Texas Select. The insurance premium was considerably lower than other insurers for the same coverage. But in 2006, the company went bankrupt, and I had to switch to another insurer at a higher premium. Texas Select's low rate may have worked on a very small group of well-qualified customers, but being too aggressive with pricing drove the insurance company out of business.

In his 2004 shareholder letter, Buffett called Berkshire Hathaway subsidiary National Indemnity Company a "disciplined underwriter" because from 1986 through 1999 the company would not match its "most optimistic competitor" on pricing and was willing to lose customers to maintain its underwriting profitability.[2]

If a company tries to gain customers without watching its bottom line, stay away.

It Faces Regulatory Landscape Shifts

For many years, for-profit education was a lucrative business, as it provided career training and college-level education to people who would otherwise not qualify for accredited colleges and universities. Revenue and profit were soaring for decades, and for-profit educators' stocks were among the best performers during the first decade of this century. But suddenly everything came to a stop. Their students could not find jobs and were deep in debt with student loans. And the government, having provided billions in financial aid, is on the hook for the loss with student loans. For-profit education companies are under investigation by the government, and new laws were established that would greatly limit their capability of enrolling new students. The industry collapsed and shareholders lost big.

Be sure to consider the regulatory risk with the companies in which you invest. After the financial crisis in 2008, new laws were enacted to regulate the banking industry. Many revenue sources disappeared. Hospitals and healthcare insurers have had to do business differently after Obamacare became law. These are the risks involved in investing in regulated industries.

It Becomes Aged

A company being aged does not necessarily mean that it is in business for too many years. It means that the company cannot adapt to the shift of the industry dynamics; its products have lost their appeal and are replaced by new technologies. Newspapers, once dominant news providers and advertisers in the areas they serve, are now being displaced by the Internet. Blockbuster, the brick-and-mortar store that rented video DVDs, was replaced by Netflix. Kodak's film was replaced by digital cameras. And retail stores have been replaced by online shopping.

Canadian smartphone maker BlackBerry once dominated the corporate world and had more than 50 percent of the smartphone market share. Every executive in the corporate world had a BlackBerry. Even I used two BlackBerry phones. But the company was too slow to adapt to touchscreen phones, and it never built an ecosystem that would increase the switching cost for customers. I remember the days when I could never memorize the combination of keys on BlackBerry to delete blocks of emails. Now BlackBerry is a forgotten player in the smartphone market.

The problem with these aged companies is that they do own a lot of assets: real estate, patents, brands, business subsidiaries, and so on, and those can look attractive to value investors after the stock has declined by a large percentage. But often they are value traps, and this is where value investors lose most of their money. I will discuss value traps in greater detail in the next section of this chapter.

■ ■ ■

If the warning signs in the previous chapter are the symptoms of the disease, the behaviors discussed in this section are the internal problems that cause the disease. A company that displays the warning signs of the last chapter is not necessarily sick. You can still buy these companies if you understand the reason behind the signs and take these into consideration for purchase price. But if a company is displaying the behavior that I just described, it should be altogether avoided.

The tricky part is that these companies don't necessarily fail quickly. Although they are actually "dead companies walking," as termed by hedge fund manager Scott Fearon in his excellent book that carries the same name,[3] they can continue to exist for years, especially when the market is booming and funding is easy to find. They can be enticing to those who look for price bargains. But, as Peter Lynch said, "Just because a company is doing poorly doesn't mean it can't do worse."[4] With these companies, things can get much worse.

Value Traps

An experienced value investor can recognize most of the bad business behaviors described in the last section. But unfortunately for value investors, a price bargain is often so attractive that it blinds them from looking at the long-term prospect of the business value. This price bargain can be a value trap in which the business keeps eroding value. Value investors lose far more money by falling into value traps than by paying too much to buy stocks. Even some of the best value investors can tumble into value traps. Berkshire Hathaway was a value trap at the time of Buffett's purchase, which eventually cost him and his partners $100 billion.[5] Sears, as I discussed extensively in Chapter 2, is a value trap that cost Bruce Berkowitz and his Fairholme Fund shareholders many years of outperformance.

In value traps, the stock price does usually look cheap relative to the earnings, cash flow, and especially the assets of the company. These assets can be real estate, patents, the brands, the collections, or the businesses the company owns. But the company has lost its competitive advantage and is on the path of permanent decline in its earnings power. It may seem that even if the company does not earn any money, its stock price is still a bargain relative to the assets it owns. But in reality, there is rarely a catalyst that can force the company into a quick liquidation. The first choice for management is always to turn the business around. The process can drag on for years, and in the meantime, the value of the business continues to decline. Even if it enters a fire sale, the assets can rarely fetch prices close to their worth, and the liquidation cost can also eat into a large percentage of the proceeds.

I commented on BlackBerry in the previous section. The involvement in BlackBerry by large value investment firms Primecap Management and Fairfax Financial in the past several years is a typical case of value investors falling into a value trap. Both investment firms have been in business for decades and have built enviable track records. Neither of them bought BlackBerry during its fast-growth stage when its stock was traded at high valuations. The stock reached its peak at close to $150 per share or $80 billion in market cap in 2008. These firms started to buy in 2010 after the stock lost about half from its peak and looked cheap. But the stock price kept slipping and both firms kept adding to their shares. By 2012, the stock was traded below $17 and looked even cheaper relative to the company's assets. The rationale behind the investment is that the company had valuable assets and a sizable business that included:

> ... the brand name, a security system second to none, a distribution network across 650 telecom carriers worldwide, a 79 million subscriber base, enterprise customers accounting for 90 percent of the Fortune 500, almost exclusive usage by governments in Canada, the United States and the U.K., a huge original patent portfolio, an outstanding new operating system developed by QNX and $2.9 billion in cash with no debt.[6]

In 2013, BlackBerry hired Thorsten Heins as new CEO to turn the business around. It didn't work out. In less than a year it hired John Chen to replace Heins. The Caltech-trained Chen had an impressive resume of running technology companies.[7] But since he joined, BlackBerry has declined from "revenues of approximately $8 billion with cash of $2.6 billion and no debt" to "revenues of less than $1.5 billion with cash of $1.2 billion and debt of $600 million." Its tangible book value per share has shrunk from $12.5 in February 2012 to $1.72 as of November 2016. The company has been losing money every year of the last four.[8] The stock is now traded at $7. If measured by price/tangible-book-value, the stock is now more expensive at $7 than it was at $17 in 2012.

One may argue that BlackBerry's 4,000-plus patent portfolio alone is worth more than its current book value of $1.72 per share. This might be true. When Apple and Microsoft bought the patents of defunct Nortel in 2011, or Google purchased Motorola Mobility for its patents in 2013, they paid over $7,000 for each patent. But patents are hard to value. When I was still a scientist with my former employer, our legal counsel told me that during patent lawsuits both sides print their patents and bring the printouts to court to compare the height of their stacks of patents. The company with the higher stack wins the suit. It simply costs too much to get into the details of patent claims. And, oh boy, reading patent documents is the most boring work in the world. For the Nortel patents, Google initially wanted to pay just $1,500 per patent. As time progresses, many of the patents will reach their 20-year protection lifetime and become worthless. Talk about the erosion of value!

The key to identifying a value trap is to check if the company's competitive advantage still exists and if the company can still grow its value. Once the business loses its competitive advantage and is on the decline, its assets also lose their earnings power and will be worth far less. Investors should always ask themselves these questions: Can the business still make money in the way it once did? Are there competitors that now do what the company does but better? Can competitors make money by offering similar products and services at lower prices?

Weight Watchers is another example of a costly value trap. The stock was traded at above $80 in 2011 and the market cap was above $5 billion. Internet, free mobile, and other weight-management apps and electronic weight-management approaches competed for Weight Watchers' business at a much lower cost. The company has experienced a long-term trend of shrinking profit margins. Investors who paid attention to its profit margins had plenty of opportunities to get out of the stock. Today the stock is traded at just above $10.

Amazon CEO Jeff Bezos famously said that "your margin is my opportunity."[9] If a business cannot build an economic moat to protect its profitability, its profit margins are destined to shrink due to competition.

The decline of value traps can happen in four stages:

Stage 1. Gross margin and operating margin decline. If a company loses its competitive advantage, its margins usually decline first. At this stage, its revenue and profit may continue to increase, which may mask the company's problem. This is where Weight Watchers was during the years 2000 through 2006.

Stage 2. As revenue growth slows, earnings stop growing. This is where Weight Watchers was from 2006 through 2012.

Stage 3. As revenue growth slows further, earnings start to decline. This is where Weight Watchers was from 2012 through 2013.

Stage 4. Both revenue and earnings decline. This is where Weight Watchers has been since 2013.

For fast-changing industries like smartphones, the declines happen much faster and each stage is shorter than it was for Weight

Watchers. The worst loss to stock prices happens when the company's margins and earnings are on the decline and the company is on its way to losing money. The stock may look cheap, but an investor who worries more about the competitiveness of the business than the price bargain will not get into this kind of situation. In October 2015, it was reported that Oprah Winfrey bought 10 percent of Weight Watchers; the stock jumped 300 percent on the news. Oprah is now advertising for the company and sharing her own experience with the company's weight-loss program. But the key is if her fans will follow her and become paying members, which is yet to be seen. Weight Watchers' competitors still cost far less, and that fact cannot be changed by Oprah. Even a good captain cannot save a sinking ship, never mind a celebrity.

Many of the value traps eventually fail completely. Some may be able to reinvent themselves and change their product focus and stabilize at lower levels. The latter case might be seen as a turnaround and the stocks may recover slightly, but they can rarely regain their past glory. In either case, the loss to those who buy them for the price bargain during the decline is permanent.

Options, Margins, and Shorts

At the beginning of this chapter, I suggested playing with stock options, buying on margins, and shorting stocks as sure ways to lose money. If you buy the stock of a good company, time is on your side. But the same cannot be said for the stock options of the same company. With stock options, you are predicting the movement of the stock prices of the company for certain time periods. Even if you are right about the direction of the company's value, the stock price can move against you and you can lose it all.

Buying on margin has a similar effect. Your gain and loss are amplified by the margin. During an extreme market swing, you may lose it all, even if your opinion on the company is correct.

When you short stocks, your maximum gain is 100 percent, while your maximum loss is infinite. Though many companies die and their stocks move to zero, very few people can make money shorting stocks for a prolonged duration because over the long term the economy and business grow and the stock market has a bias for moving higher. Maybe you are right that the company is in trouble and could one day go into bankruptcy, but it can take a long time for its stock to go down. Few executives want to see their stocks go down. They may use techniques such as share buybacks and dividend raises to drive up the stock price. In stock market bubbles, even a company that keeps losing money can see its stock going up and up. In the meantime, you have to pay the borrowing cost and pay back the dividends to those you borrow the shares from. Remember what John Keynes said: "Markets can remain irrational a lot longer than you can remain solvent." You want to avoid situations in which time works against you and you face the possibility of permanent loss.

The only time you should consider using options is probably selling put options on the stock you intend to buy and for which you hope to reduce the share cost. A put option is a contract in which the option seller, who collects the option premium, is obligated to buy the stock at the exercise price (strike price) before the expiration of the contract. If at the time of exercise, the stock is traded lower than the strike price, the put seller is paying a higher price than the market price. If instead the stock is traded higher than the strike price, the put buyer (owner) will not exercise the option and the contract will expire worthless. Buffett sold put options to lower his purchase cost when he wanted to buy Coca-Cola stocks in 1993 and Burlington Northern Santa Fe (BNSF) stocks in 2008.

We can look at the details of Buffett's put transactions on BNSF to understand how to lower the share cost when buying stocks by selling puts, as shown in the table below.

All the put options that Buffett sold on BNSF are short term—about two months. For the transaction on 10/6/2008, the stock was traded at $84.98 per share. Buffett could have bought the stock outright at that price. But instead he sold put options with the strike price of $80 and the expiration date in two months for $7.02 per share. By the expiration of the put options on 12/8/2008, the stock was traded at $76.55. Buffett had to buy the stock at $80. But his real cost per share is $72.98, which is equal to the strike price minus the option price. So, Buffett reduced his share cost by $12 by selling puts instead of buying the stock outright on the day of the option transaction. Buffett continued to do this in multiple transactions until December 2008 and bought 7.8 million shares of BNSF along the way, saving $75 million for Berkshire Hathaway on those shares, which is a significant 13.7 percent of the total cost.

Transaction Date	Market Price ($)	Strike Price ($)	Shares Sold	Date Exercisable	Option Price ($)	Share Cost After Option Exercised	Price on Date of Exercise ($)	Money Saved per Share ($)	Total Saved Relative to Buying Stocks on Traction Date ($)
10/6/2008	84.98	80	1,309,524	12/8/2008	7.02	72.98	76.55	12	15,714,288
10/8/2008	81.44	80	1,190,476	12/9/2008	7.03	72.97	75.2	8.47	10,083,332
10/8/2008	81.44	77	761,111	12/9/2008	5.78	71.22	75.2	10.22	7,778,554
10/10/2008	80.16	75	1,217,500	12/12/2008	7.09	67.91	74.68	12.25	14,914,375
10/16/2008	80.47	76	1,000,000	12/19/2008	6.2	69.8	74.68	10.67	10,670,000
12/3/2008	75.5	75	2,325,000	1/30/2009	6.35	68.65	66.25	6.85	15,926,250
								Total Saved:	75,086,799

Of course, there is no free lunch. This case worked in Buffett's favor because during the months after he sold the put options, BNSF stock went down. If it had gone up instead, Buffett would not have gotten the shares. He would have simply pocketed the $51 million in option premiums. But those shares would have eventually cost $105 million more when Berkshire Hathaway acquired BNSF at $100 per share in February 2010. Therefore, there is always a chance that you will not get to buy the stock at the price on the option transaction date, and you will lose the investment opportunity if you don't want to pay a higher price.

Another reason selling BNSF options worked well for Buffett was timing. Although Buffett said he doesn't time the market, he sure knows when to sell options. The third quarter of 2008 through the first quarter of 2009 was the most volatile time for the stock market in more than three decades except Black Monday in 1987. When volatility is high, option premium is high. Two-month put options with a strike price 5 percent lower than the stock price carried a premium of close to 9 percent. Today, similar put options can only fetch a premium of around 1 percent.

When selling put options, you always have the possibility to buy the stocks when the contract expires. Therefore, you must make sure that you only sell put options on the stocks you want to own for the long term, and that you have the cash to buy the stock. If the stock prices go lower than the strike price, you will get the shares. If you love the option premium but hate the stock, you will get yourself into big trouble. I personally know someone who sold puts on Nortel stocks. She got to pocket the option premium but was forced to buy the Nortel shares, which eventually went to zero!

In summary, selling put options can be an effective way to reduce the share cost. But do remember:

- Work with short-term put options.
- It works well when market volatility is high.
- Do so only with the companies you want to buy and that you have the cash to buy.
- You may lose the investment opportunity altogether if the stock price goes up.

Otherwise, stay away from options, margins, and shorts.

■ ■ ■

If I made buying good companies sound simple in Chapters 3 and 4, I have probably made it sound too complex in the preceding and current chapters. Of course, it is not simple. Charlie Munger said that anyone who considers it simple is stupid. But we can look for situations that are relatively simple, a company with a business that is easy to understand, and an industry that changes relatively slowly and has a minimal regulatory risk. Buffett said that in investing, you don't get rewarded more by working on difficult moves like in gymnastics. He uses three jars—"yes," "no," and "too-hard"—when he looks at each investment opportunity. Most of the ideas belong in the too-hard jar.

If it still sounds too hard, don't get discouraged. You can participate in the long-term prosperity of good business and achieve satisfactory returns by investing in a basket of great companies. And it is *really* simple.

8

Passive Portfolios, Cash Level, and Performance

I f you have made it to this point in the book, you probably realize that there is no secret to investing. Once in a while, I come across someone expressing the wish that Warren Buffett reveal his investing secrets to the public. Buffett has revealed *all* his investing secrets over and over throughout the last 60 years in his shareholder letters, interviews, speeches, and writing; they are there for everyone to grab—you just need to be willing to work hard and learn.

If, however, you are not interested in studying investing, or you don't have the time, you can still benefit from the growth of great businesses by simply investing in the S&P 500 index funds, a good mutual fund, or a basket of good companies. As I demonstrated in Chapter 3, S&P 500 companies do relatively better than all other U.S. businesses on average. A cautious and survival-bias-free study by Sungarden Investment Research found that over ten-year periods, the S&P 500 index beat 60 percent of actively managed mutual funds.[1] Even Buffett said that if he died, his wife would invest in an index fund. About index investing, in his 1993 shareholder letter, Buffett wrote: "When 'dumb' money acknowledges its limitations, it ceases to be dumb."[2] S&P 500 index funds generally have low fees and low portfolio turnover. Low fees is also one of the key reasons the index funds outperformed, and low portfolio turnover makes index-fund investing more tax-efficient.

To achieve the best long-term results, you should avoid trying to time the market and should instead buy the index funds continuously, regardless of how the stock market is doing. You also need to be constantly fully invested. If so, over the long term, you will do very well. You can do even better if you invest in a basket of good companies at reasonable prices and take advantage of the benefits of long-term higher business returns of these good companies.

A Basket of Good Companies

In Chapter 3, I highlighted that if we focus our investing on the good companies that are consistently profitable and have high investment returns, we can lower the chance of losing money and achieve above-average overall returns. If we buy them at reasonable valuations, the returns should be even better. Those who do not have the time or interest to study the details of each company can instead simply buy a basket of these good companies, which should do better than index investing over time.

GuruFocus began tracking a portfolio of these companies in 2009. The portfolio consists of 25 companies that were constantly profitable during the prior ten years and were undervalued as measured by the discounted cash flow model. Following are the performances of the portfolio from January 2009 to September 2016:

Year	S&P 500	25 Undervalued Predictable Companies
2009	23.45%	55.72%
2010	12.78%	20.17%
2011	0	–3.32%
2012	13.41%	5.29%
2013	29.6%	24.81%
2014	11.39%	11.38%
2015	–0.73%	–0.17%
2016	9.54%	21.08%
Cumulative Gain	148%	220%
Annualized	12.0%	15.7%

The portfolio is rebalanced annually on the first trading day of each year. The portfolio value is calculated daily. During the year, we do nothing to the portfolio. If any of the positions are acquired, they will be converted to cash or the shares of the acquiring company, depending on the structure of the acquisition deal. Since inception on January 2, 2009, the portfolio has achieved an annualized gain of 15.7 percent. During the same period, the S&P 500 gained 12 percent a year. Therefore, the portfolio of consistently profitable companies outperformed the market by 3.7 percent per year since 2009. All numbers do not include dividends.

In January 2010, we started two other portfolios of these consistently profitable companies that are sold at close to the ten-year-price/sales low and ten-year-price/book low ratios. The performances until September 2016 are reflected below:

Year	S&P 500	Top 25 Historical Low P/S Ratio Companies	Top 25 Historical Low P/B Ratio Companies
2010	12.78%	19.05%	16.39%
2011	0	−2.01%	−1.87%
2012	13.41%	17.79%	17.62%
2013	29.6%	29.60%	33.18%
2014	11.39%	15.09%	20.01%
2015	−0.73%	−3.75%	−4.63%
2016	9.54%	19.55%	16.6%
Cumulative Gain	101%	136%	139%
Annualized	10.5%	13.0%	13.2%

Since inception, these portfolios outperformed the market by about 2.5 percent a year.

I should point out that none of these portfolios outperformed the market every year, but over time they outperformed the market average by decent margins. The performances listed above were achieved by initially investing 4 percent of the portfolio in each position. The portfolio was rebalanced once a year. At the time of rebalancing, we ran the screeners again. We do not make changes to the stocks that remain in the screen. We sell the stocks that are out of the screen and buy the new stocks in equal weight. The turnover of the portfolio was about 25 percent per year.

Compared with the Magic Formula invented by hedge fund manager Joel Greenblatt,[3] the GuruFocus approach considers the long-term performance of the businesses instead of just the latest performance as with the Magic Formula. The quality of the companies in the GuruFocus approach is higher than the quality of the stocks that passed Greenblatt's Magic Formula screen. I expect the portfolio will also perform relatively better during down markets.

Nevertheless, these three portfolios have not been tested in down cycles. Among the model portfolios tracked on GuruFocus is the portfolio of Gurus' Broadest Owned Portfolio that did well in both up and down markets. This is a portfolio of the 25 most broadly owned stocks among a selected group of investors. The portfolio is also rebalanced once a year. You can view the latest portfolio and performance at this link: http://www.gurufocus.com/model_portfolio .php?mp=largecap. The annual performance of the portfolio is listed below. It outperformed the S&P 500 index by about 2.4 percent a year on average. Since inception in January 2006 to the end of 2016, the portfolio outperformed the S&P 500 index in 9 out of the 11 years.

Year	S&P 500	Most Broadly Held Guru Portfolio
2006	13.62%	15.18%
2007	3.53%	−5.47%
2008	−38.49%	−29.98%
2009	23.45%	30.70%
2010	12.78%	14.63%
2011	0	0.54%
2012	13.41%	16.99%
2013	29.6%	30.85%
2014	11.39%	12.30%
2015	−0.73%	6.07%
2016	9.54%	0.38%
Cumulative Gain	79%	129%
Annualized	5.5%	7.8%

We can see that over the past 11 years, the portfolio has outperformed the index by a cumulative 50 percent. This is significant for the investor who is trying to accumulate wealth over the long term.

The investing approach of a basket of high-quality companies is slightly more complex than investing in index funds. You need to hold 25 positions instead of just one, but it requires only one rebalance a year, and most times the rebalance simply involves about 7 stocks of the 25 in the portfolio. The 2 percent per year in outperformance makes it worthwhile.

Dividend-Income Investing

The high-quality passive-portfolio approach can also be applied to retirement investing. An investor can build a retirement portfolio of high-quality companies and live on the dividends paid by the companies in the portfolio, never having to touch the principals of the portfolio.

For a retirement portfolio, it is extremely important that the companies in the portfolios have durable financial strength and consistent profitability so that the companies can survive the bad times, as well as continue their dividend payments. Furthermore, the companies should be able to increase their dividend payment over time so that the investors' dividend income grows faster than inflation. The portfolio should be reasonably diversified across different industries to smooth out any industry downturn.

The requirements for dividend-income portfolios can be summarized as:

1. The company needs to have a strong balance sheet. A strong balance sheet is essential to the survival of the company and the safety of dividends. In GuruFocus's scale of financial strength ranking, from 1 to 10, the financial strength needs to be 6 or higher.
2. The company needs to be highly profitable. Only when it is profitable can it generate enough cash to pay out dividends and maintain solid financial strength. In GuruFocus's scale of profitability ranking, from 1 to 10, the profitability needs to be 7 or higher.
3. The company needs to demonstrate consistent past performance and profitability. This is guaranteed through GuruFocus Predictability Rank of 2.5-star or higher.

4. The company needs to have a reasonably high return on invested capital. GuruFocus requires a ten-year median return on invested capital of 10 percent or higher. This is the requirement for high-quality companies.
5. The company needs to be 100 percent profitable over the past ten years and have the ten-year median operating margin of 10 percent or higher.
6. The company needs to show reasonable growth capability. The growth rates of revenue and earnings should be 5 percent or higher.
7. The company needs to display a commitment to dividend increases for ten years or more.
8. The dividend payout ratio should be 0.7 or less. We hope that the dividend payout ratio is low so that it has more room for dividend increases.
9. The current dividend yield should be 2 percent or higher. This is a requirement that the dividend yield is higher than the market average.
10. The five-year dividend yield on cost should be 2.5 percent or higher. Dividend on cost is defined as the ratio of the dividend paid in five years on the cost today. This requirement makes sure that the company is increasing dividends fast enough so that within five years, the dividends on the current investments generate more income than they do currently.

Requirements 1 through 6 exist to ensure that we buy only high-quality companies. Requirements 7 through 10 are used to guarantee that the companies meet the dividend requirements. I have created a screener based on these requirements with Guru-Focus's All-In-One screener; you can find it by going to GuruFocus .com Menu → All-In-One Screener → Dividend Income Screener.

The number of companies that can pass this screener is heavily dependent on the market valuation. When the market valuation is high, the average dividend yield is low and fewer stocks can pass the screener. If I run the screener today—with the stock market within 3 percent of its all-time high after seven-and-a-half years of a bull market—only 16 stocks pass the screener and they have an average dividend yield of 2.4 percent, which is about 20 percent higher than the yield of the S&P 500 index. This same screener would have seen far more stocks passing a few years ago, when the market was lower.

At the dividend yield of 2.4 percent, an investment portfolio of $1 million generates $24,000 in annual dividend income. Nevertheless, the average five-year yield-on-cost of the 16 stocks is 5.44 percent. This means that if the companies grow dividends as quickly as they did in the past five years, investors will see their dividend income more than doubled in the next five years.

Holding Cash

In the dividend-investing portfolio, I set the minimum dividend yield as 2 percent. This is low relative to the historical level. The stock market is close to the all-time high and the dividend yield is at the all-time low. If one decides to require a higher dividend yield, there will not be a sufficiently diversified list of stocks to fill the dividend portfolio. Money has to be parked in cash to wait for better opportunities.

This is also the dilemma that valuation-sensitive investors currently face. After the market has run up, the valuation of most of the stocks is full. There are not enough stocks meeting the requirements of the margin of safety. Relaxing margin-of-safety requirements means a large downside risk. Again, money has to be parked in cash to wait for better opportunities.

Disciplined and experienced investors can choose to do so and may achieve better long-term results. But it is extremely hard to hold cash as the market continues to go up and up. Holding cash drags down the overall performance of the portfolio, especially at a time when cash is paying close to nothing and "cash is trash." But when the market comes to downcycles, which it does once in a while and definitely will again in the future, holding cash protects your investments and allows you the opportunity to buy stocks at much lower prices. This is why the Yacktman Fund could outperform the S&P 500 by 11 percent in the down market of 2008 and by 33 percent in the market recovery of 2009. "Cash is king" during a down market.

When you hold cash, you still want to get some returns while maintaining the liquidity. You can buy short-term Treasury bills through TreasuryDirect or buy short-term Treasury ETFs such as iShares 1–3 Year Treasury Bond ETF SHY. The ETF, however, does come with some interest-rate risk.

You can sometimes get higher returns for the cash by engaging in merger arbitrage activities, which Buffett did frequently in his earlier years.[4]

Merger Arbitrage

When Buffett had more cash than investing ideas, he engaged in merger arbitrages to achieve higher returns than Treasury bills. This kept him from relaxing standards for long-term investments and "kept him out of bars," in Charlie Munger's words. He continued to do this until at least the mid-1990s.[5]

With merger arbitrage, if Company A is acquiring Company B, investors short the stocks of Company A and simultaneously long the stocks of Company B in an equivalent number of shares. If the merger goes through, the shares will cancel each other and the investor pockets the price spread that existed at the time of the trades.

Sometimes mergers are cash deals. That is, Company B is acquired by Company A for cash. In this case, there is no need to short Company A stock. Investors just need to buy Company B stock at the discount from the announced deal price.

The biggest risk with merger arbitrage is when the merger falls through. Usually, during mergers, Company A offers a large premium for the stocks of Company B. After the merger announcement, the price of Company B stocks immediately jumps and is now close to the offer price. If the merger falls through, Company B stock will fall right away to where it was or even lower. The investors who look for making perhaps just 2 percent on the price spread will see a loss of maybe 40 percent or higher. In this case, the investors have to sell the Company B shares at a deep loss to prevent a failed short-term investment from becoming a long-term burden. Therefore, if only one out of 20 merger arbitrages fails, the investor makes no money.

Sometimes there are also pleasant surprises. After the merger announcement, another company may also want to buy Company B. They will need to offer a higher price. This bidding war can lift the stock of Company B even more. So, instead of just getting 2 to 3 percent, you may get 20 percent or higher returns in a very short time. This is an "I am feeling lucky!" moment with merger arbitrage.

But there are far more broken deals than pleasant surprises. Because of the disparity of risk between gain and loss, the key to merger arbitrage is to avoid bad deals. Both Buffett and hedge fund manager John Paulson had great success with merger arbitrage.[6] They both follow strict rules to avoid the deals that might go bad. These are some of the things to consider before getting into a position:

- Is this from a large acquirer?
- Does the acquirer have a good track record of closing deals?
- Is the merger agreement definitive?
- Is the deal subject to financing conditions?
- Is the deal subject to due diligence?
- Is the company being acquired by a solid performer?
- How reasonable is the valuation?
- What is the regulatory risk?
- What is the tax consequence?
- What is the chance of another bidder coming in to sweeten the deal?

Even with these considerations, many other things can happen to break a deal: market conditions, interest rates, politics, another bidder, and so forth. Investors need to diversify their activities across different industries.

Merger arbitrage is for sophisticated investors only. Interested investors can read Paulson's "The 'Risk' in Risk Arbitrage" in *Managing Hedge Fund Risk*, compiled by Virginia Reynolds Parker.[7]

How to Look at the Performances

Increasing the cash level in the portfolio when the valuation is high and reducing it when the valuation is low doesn't necessarily generate higher long-term returns because it is impossible to know how long an overvalued market can stay overvalued. You may get into cash too early during a bull market and miss gains, and you may reduce the cash level too late and again miss gains.

When it comes to looking at the performance of an investing strategy, the biggest mistake investors make is usually looking in the rearview mirror. They make their decisions based on the strategy's performance in the near past and tend to put their money into the investments that did well lately. This is also how most investors treat mutual funds and ETFs. At the end of the 1990s, many investors switched to the technology sector because the technology funds did far better in the preceding several years. The problem is that the technology sector outperformance lifted the valuation of the sector and positioned it for lower future returns. This is the case for all funds and strategies that concentrate their portfolios in certain sectors, regions, or asset classes.

Investors should look at a fund or a strategy's performances during at least one full market cycle to decide if it is working. This is true for sector funds and region funds. It is also true for funds or strategies that focus in any industry or asset class. If the market continues to go up, the funds which have chosen not to be fully invested all the time will underperform. But if the market goes down, these funds will outperform, as they may take advantage of the lower valuations during market corrections with the cash in hand. This is why the previously mentioned study by Sungarden Investment Research found that during the past two bull markets, the S&P 500 index outperformed 80 percent and 63 percent of its peers. However, during the down-market cycles, the index beat only 34 percent and 38 percent of its actively managed counterparts.

A full market cycle here means from peak to peak or trough to trough. The last two peak-to-peak full cycles are from the first quarter of 2000 to the third quarter of 2007, and until about now, the first quarter of 2017. The current bull market that started in March 2009 may still last, but it should currently be very close to its peak.

■ ■ ■

In summary, even if you are not interested or don't have the time to research companies, you can still benefit from the long-term prosperity of great businesses by investing in a basket of good companies. You do need to stick to a strategy and stay fully invested all the time and buy on a dollar-cost average basis. You will do considerably better over time with this strategy than with index funds.

For those who enjoy researching businesses and companies, you can do even better by concentrating your investments on a handful of good companies. There is no secret. Once you are in the framework of buying good companies at fair prices, the only things you need to do are learn about the business and work hard.

CHAPTER 9

How to Evaluate Companies

In Chapter 2, I discussed the valuation methods based on the assets of companies. In Chapter 5, I focused on the valuation method based on the free cash flow and the earnings of the companies that have predictable earnings power. In this chapter, I want to explain business evaluation, in general, and how different evaluation methods can or cannot be applied to businesses across different industries and in different situations.

This chapter offers a broad explanation of valuation methods and their applications. Although I have previously mentioned that some industries should be avoided by investors who seek to invest in only good companies, some of these industries will be remarked on in this chapter. So, please don't confuse the comments in this chapter with the investing philosophy of buying only good companies.

Valuation approaches can be divided into three categories: (1) valuation ratios, (2) intrinsic values, and (3) rate of return. I will discuss each of them in detail in this chapter.

Valuation Ratio Approach

Valuation ratio approach is the most commonly used method of valuation. Among all the valuation ratios, P/E is the most popularly used ratio. Then there are price/sales, price/book, price/free-cash-flow, EV/EBIT, EV/EBITDA, and many others.

P/E Ratio

The P/E ratio can be viewed as the number of years it takes for the company to earn back the price that investors paid for the stock. For example, if a company earns $2 per share per year, and the stock is traded at $30, the P/E ratio is 15. Therefore, it takes 15 years for the investor to earn back the $30 paid for the stock through the company's earnings, assuming the earnings stay constant over the next 15 years.

In real business, earnings never stay unchanged. If a company grows its earnings, it takes fewer years for the investor to earn back the cost of buying the stock. If a company's earnings decline, it takes additional years. As a shareholder, you want the company to earn back the price that you paid as quickly as possible. Therefore, lower P/E stocks are more attractive than higher P/E stocks, as long as the P/E ratio is positive. Also, for the stocks with the same P/E ratio, the faster-growing business is more attractive.

The fair P/E ratio of a stock is about the growth rate of the company, according to Peter Lynch.[1] In Chapter 5, I explained that at the fair P/E ratio, the stock price for a growing company is approximately at its fair value, and the fair price is affected by interest rates.

It is useful to look at the historical range of a company's P/E and see where it stands compared with historical valuations. For example, Figure 9.1 shows the P/E ratio of Wal-Mart since 1998. Investors who bought the stock in 2000, when the P/E ratio was at an all-time high of 60, did not recover their loss until Wal-Mart nearly quadrupled its earnings per share 12 years later. But investors who bought at the all-time low P/E of 11 in 2011 were rewarded quickly with a gain of more 40 percent in 12 months.

If a company loses money, the P/E ratio becomes meaningless. As I pointed out in Chapter 3, avoiding money-losing companies can boost returns.

To compare the stocks with different growth rates, Lynch invented a ratio called PEG, which is defined as P/E ratio divided by the growth rate. It seems that when PEG = 1, the stock is fair valued. He still said he would rather buy a company growing 20 percent a year with a P/E of 20 than a company growing 10 percent a year with a P/E of 10.[2]

Figure 9.1   WMT P/E

Because P/E ratio measures how long it takes to earn back the price the investor paid, P/E ratio can be used to compare the valuation of the stocks across businesses from different industries. That is why it is the most important and widely used indicator for the valuation of stocks.

P/E ratio can be affected by nonrecurring items such as the sale of a part of the business, a onetime assets write-down, and so on. This may dramatically affect the reported earnings for the current year or quarter. But it does not repeat. Investors need to pay attention to this when using P/E to value companies.

Investors also need to be aware that P/E ratio can be misleading when the underlying business is cyclical and unpredictable. P/E ratio works best for the companies with steady earnings. Cyclical businesses have higher profit margins at the peaks of business cycles and lower margins or even losses at the bottoms of business cycles. Their earnings are high at the peaks of the cycles and their stock P/E ratios are artificially low. A good example is Southwest Airlines, the second largest airline by market cap. Its P/E ratio from 1998 to 2016 is reflected in Figure 9.2.

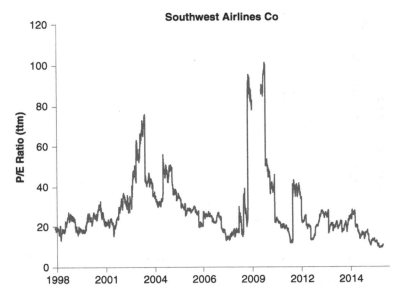

Figure 9.2   LUV P/E

Apparently Southwest Airlines' P/E ratio was the highest during the cycle troughs of 2003 and 2009, though its stock had lost 50 percent from its previous peaks. It seemed cheap as of September 2016, as the stock was traded at the P/E ratio of under 10. But its recent earnings are pumped up by both low oil prices and the decent economy, and may not be sustainable if oil prices go up or the economy slows down. Its historical earnings per share are shown in Figure 9.3.

Clearly the earnings have dramatically deviated from the historical trend since 2014, when oil prices started to drop. The unusually high earnings have made the P/E of the stock low, although the stock price is close to an all-time high. The better ratio for evaluating cyclical businesses is price/sales ratio.

EV/EBIT and EV/EBITDA are the variations of P/E, where EV stands for enterprise value, EBIT stands for earnings before interest and tax, and EBITDA stands for earnings before interest, tax, depreciation and amortization. Arguably, they are better valuation ratios than P/E because enterprise value is the true price the investor pays, given that as a shareholder, he or she owns the cash but is liable for

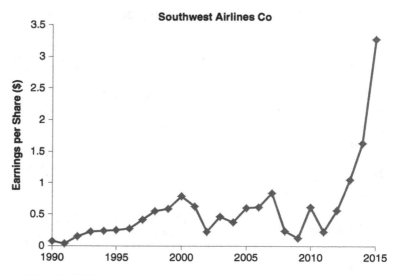

Figure 9.3   LUV EPS

the debt of the company. Furthermore, the earnings before interest and tax are less susceptible to the manipulations of the company's accounting practices.

Peter Lynch Earnings Line

Related to P/E ratio, Lynch likes to superpose the price chart with a line that is at 15 times trailing-12-month earnings and compare the relative positions of the two lines. He called this line the earnings line, which is now better known as the *Peter Lynch Earnings Line*. The chart with the price line and the earnings line is now known as the *Peter Lynch Chart*, as popularized by GuruFocus.com. In his excellent book, *One Up on Wall Street*, Lynch used many of these charts to illustrate the valuation of stocks. He wrote:

> A quick way to tell if a stock is overpriced is to compare the price line to the earnings line. If you bought familiar growth companies—such as Shoney's, The Limited, or Marriott—when the stock price fell well below the earnings line, and sold them when the stock price rose dramatically above it, the chances are you'd do pretty well.[3]

An example of the Peter Lynch Chart is illustrated in Figure 9.4 for General Dynamics Corp. (GD).

Figure 9.4   GD Peter Lynch Chart

We can see that historically when GD's stock prices fell below the earnings line, it always came back to cross it and go above it. Just as Lynch said, an investor could do pretty well by buying GD stock when its price dropped below the earnings line and selling when it rose above. This technique can be applied to many stocks, especially those with a steady long-term earnings trend.

The Peter Lynch Chart does have limitations due to its earnings lines being drawn at fixed P/E = 15, which does not fit even for blue-chip stocks like CVS Health Corp., PepsiCo Inc., Johnson & Johnson, and Procter & Gamble. A better earnings line is the one drawn at its historical median P/E ratio instead of at the fixed number of 15. This historical median P/E can be different for different stocks. For example, in the case of CVS, the better earnings line is drawn at P/E = 18.6. The earnings line with P/E = 15 is almost always below the price line. (See Figure 9.5.)

The reason the appropriate earnings line is higher is probably because the interest rate in the past decade has been much lower than it was during Lynch's time at Fidelity. The lower interest rate lifted the nominal valuations of all stocks.

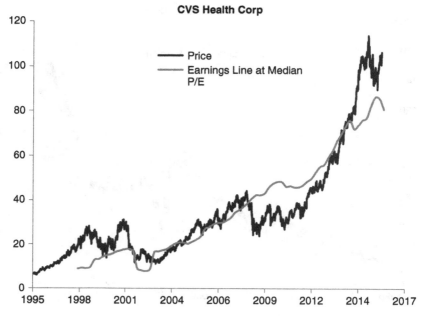

Figure 9.5   CVS Median P/E Chart

In addition to the earnings line drawn at fair P/E, we can also draw earnings lines at both the lowest and the highest P/E within its history. For instance, the next chart is again for CVS, with the earnings line drawn at its lowest P/E of 10.4 and the highest P/E of 27 since 2004. Clearly, if one buys when the price line is close to the lowest P/E earnings line, and sells when the price line is close to the highest P/E earnings line, one can do extremely well. (See Figure 9.6.)

By the way, you can find all the historical P/E, earnings per share, and Peter Lynch Charts, as well as many others, by using the Interactive Chart feature at GuruFocus's website, GuruFocus.com.

Again, the Peter Lynch Chart and the variation with earnings line at median P/E ratio work well for the companies with steady growth and earnings trends, or the stalwarts, as coined by Lynch.[4] These companies tend to be found in sectors such as consumer staples, healthcare, and utilities, where the consumption of the product or service is relatively independent of economic conditions.

The Peter Lynch Chart does not work well with the sectors that are cyclical: industrials, chemicals, durable goods, and so forth.

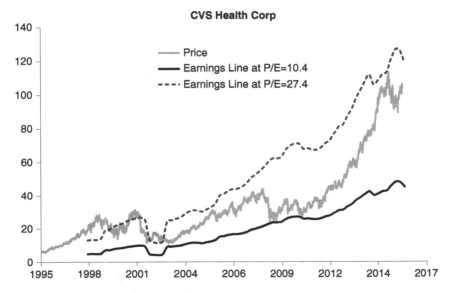

Figure 9.6   CVS Max/Min P/E Chart

In the example of Southwest Airlines, it seems that the stock price has room to go up because its current all-time-high price is far below the earnings line drawn at historical median P/E of 23.25, as shown in Figure 9.7. But its earnings line may come down quickly if either the oil price goes up or travel slows down. For cyclical companies, price/sales ratio paints a more accurate picture in terms of historical valuations.

Price/Sales Ratio

P/S ratio is an excellent valuation indicator if you want to compare a stock with its historical valuations or with other stocks in the same industry. It does not measure how long it takes for investors to get paid back like P/E ratio does; it gives only a relative valuation. P/S ratio is a great tool for evaluating cyclical businesses where P/E ratio works poorly. It works better for cyclical companies when, over time, the company's profit margin reverts to the mean. Again, in the example of Southwest Airlines, although its earnings have had many ups and downs, like a rollercoaster, the company's revenue has been going up relatively steadily. If we replace the median P/E earnings line with the median P/S earnings line in the Peter Lynch Chart,

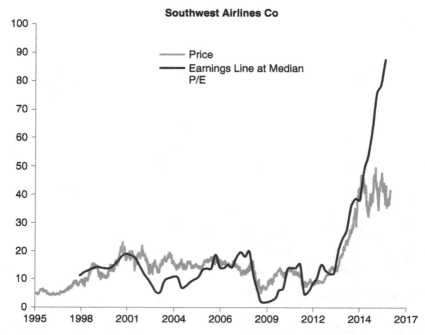

Figure 9.7   LUV Median P/E Chart

the chart clearly shows when it is a good time to buy the stock and when it is a good time to get out, as shown in Figure 9.8. In the early 2000s, the stock was traded at far above the median sales line. It took more than 14 years for those who bought in 2000 to break even. Those who bought when the stock prices were far below the median sales line in 2009 and 2011 were rewarded with outsized gains over the next 5 years. The previous chart drawn with the median P/E earnings line isn't able to provide such clear direction. Currently, Southwest Airlines looks fair valued as measured against its historical median price/sales ratio.

Similar to what we do with the earnings line, we can draw the sales lines at the highest P/S ratio and the lowest P/S ratio within certain historical periods. These lines form a band of the historical P/S ratios and can give direction to investors regarding when the stock is at a low valuation and it is a good time to buy.

This P/S bands approach works for both steadily performing companies and cyclical companies. The two charts in Figures 9.9

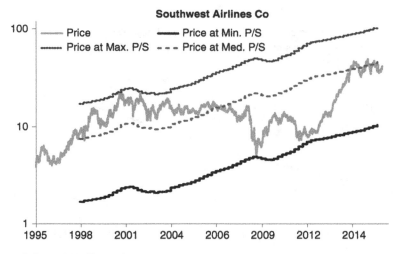

Figure 9.8   LUV P/S Bands

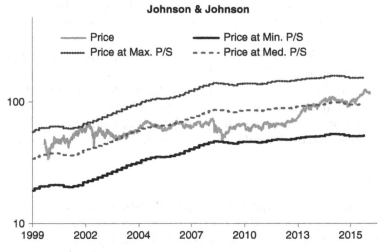

Figure 9.9   JNJ P/S Bands

and 9.10 show the P/S bands for Johnson & Johnson and Amazon. Drugmaker Johnson & Johnson's stock price has been fluctuating at about 3.5 times its revenue per share; online retailer Amazon's stock price has been traded at about 2.25 times its revenue per share.

The P/S bands approach does not work for companies that are in permanent decline and may see their P/S ratios fall all the way

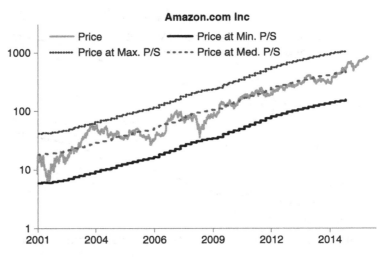

Figure 9.10   AMZN P/S Bands

to zero. And it does not work for commodity producers such as oil companies, steelmakers, goldminers, and so on, which I will discuss later in this chapter.

When P/S ratio is applied to the entire stock market, it can be used to evaluate the broad market valuation and the projected returns. In this case, the price is the total market cap of all the stocks that are traded, and sales are the GDP of the country. This is how Warren Buffett estimates the broad market valuation and projects future returns. I will explain in more detail in the next chapter.

Price/Book Ratio

Unlike the valuation ratios P/E and P/S, which are the price relative to the earnings power, P/B ratio measures the valuation of the stock relative to the equity of the company. It does not suggest anything about the operation of the company. Instead, it compares the price and the underlying assets of the company.

Benjamin Graham liked to compare the stock price with the book value of the shares and buy the ones that were sold at below book value, that is, P/B < 1. P/B ratio works well for the companies that are asset heavy and whose earnings power comes mainly from the business's tangible assets.

For the businesses that are asset light, such as software companies or insurance agencies, P/B ratio does not work well. Companies like Moody's and AutoZone have negative equity, so P/B ratio cannot be applied to them.

Price/book ratio works best for financial companies (e.g., banks and insurance companies), which deserve more detailed consideration.

P/B Ratio and Financial Companies

For financial services companies such as banks and insurance agencies, the most useful valuation parameter is price/book ratio. Financial companies follow mark-to-market accounting rules. They are required to record their assets at the fair values traded in the market. Most of the assets of financial companies are traded in the market and have market prices. The balance sheet items such as assets and liabilities reflect their current market values. Therefore, the shareholders' equity on the balance sheet of financial companies is very close to the net worth of the companies' assets in the current market.

One can also try to value a bank or insurance company based on its earnings power. But for financial companies, it's very hard to distinguish the items that are needed for calculation: the change of working capital, capital expenditures, debt, and so on. Furthermore, banks and insurance companies' true profit and loss can be very different from their reported earnings. The provision for loan loss in banks and the loss reserve with insurance companies are quite subjective, and they drastically affect the reported earnings. The true earnings from their current business activities are usually unknown until many years later, when the loan default or insurance loss happens during bad economic times.

Although it seems that we don't value the earnings power of financial companies if we just look at their book values, in fact most of their earnings power is already reflected in the prices of their assets, whether they are bonds, stocks, mortgages, or other marketable securities. A bond can sell at above or below its face value depending on changes in the interest rate and credit quality. Mortgages are sold from one bank to another at the prices that reflect their ability to generate profit.

Therefore, the book value is a rather accurate measure of net worth for financial companies. That is why the change of per-share book value is always the first thing Buffett writes about in his annual shareholder letters. Especially in Berkshire Hathaway's earlier years, its insurance operation was a much larger segment of the company, and Buffett thought the book value was a good proxy of the intrinsic value of the shares. As Berkshire acquired more large non-insurance operations such as Burlington Northern Santa Fe, Iscar, Mid-American Energy, and so on, its intrinsic value deviated more from its book value. Figure 9.11 shows the stock price of Berkshire Hathaway relative to its historical P/B bands formed by prices at maximum, median, and minimum P/B ratios. The chart gives a clear indication of the valuation of the stock and when is a good time to buy.

When evaluating financial companies with their book values, be wary about the quality of the book. Although book value comes mostly from the current market values of the assets, the market can be drastically wrong with the prices of the underlying assets. When bank loans start to default more than expected, or insurance losses come higher than anticipated at underwriting, the market prices of their assets can go down quickly. That was what happened during the 2008 financial crisis and how Dr. Michael Burry made a killing betting against mortgage-backed securities.

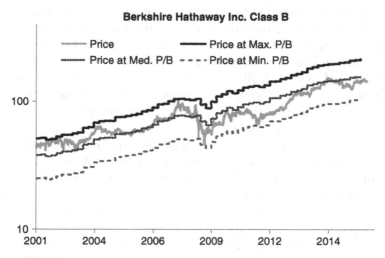

Figure 9.11   BRK P/B Bands

Therefore, when it comes to investing in financial stocks, the salient factors are the quality of the book, the growth of the book value, and the price/book ratio. Those with high-quality books and low price/book ratios are more attractively valued.

Commodity Producers

None of the above ratios work particularly well for commodity producers, the companies whose products are used by other businesses or consumers. These products include oil and gas and metals such as steel, copper, gold, and so on; they also include eggs, corn, and other grains. These companies are usually asset-heavy, and their assets are a good indication of their earnings power and net worth.

Though the products of various commodity producers are diverse in how they are produced and consumed, they share a common element: Their prices are unpredictable and can swing up and down and are out of the control of these companies. Their production costs are relatively independent of the prices of their products. Therefore, their revenue and profit are both highly dependent on the prices of the commodity they produce.

This is the case even for companies as mature as Exxon Mobile, which has a relatively diversified product portfolio and geographic distribution. Figure 9.12 shows its quarterly net income and the crude oil prices, which are closely correlated.

The strong dependence of the revenue and profit on the unpredictable commodity prices makes it very hard to value commodity producers. Investing in commodity producers is even more tricky because the commodity cycle is not necessarily synchronized with economic and stock market cycles. So, we may have low commodity prices and poor earnings for the commodity producers yet continued inflated prices for their stocks.

Ratios such as P/E and P/S cannot give us a good indication of even the relative valuations of these companies. Similarly, valuation methods such as DCF cannot give intrinsic value estimates with meaningful accuracy as the results are highly dependent on prices of the commodity in the past and the future. Even the average within the previous cycles cannot be used to predict the average of the next cycle. Any attempt of intrinsic value will result in a wide range that is a function of the future prices of the commodity. For an example, Wall

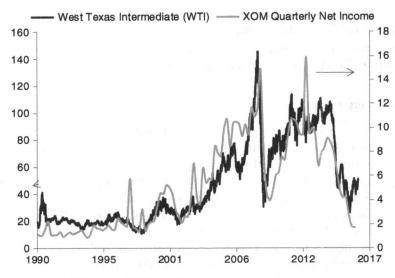

Figure 9.12   Oil Price vs. XOM Net Income

Street analysts have 18 different price targets on the stock of United States Steel, ranging for a high of $37 to a low of $7 while the stock was traded at $16, according to Barron's.[5]

An alternative measure of the valuation of commodity producers is to look at the Shiller P/E ratio of the stocks. Shiller P/E ratio was developed by Yale professor Robert Shiller for measuring the valuation of the S&P 500 index.[6] We have adopted the methodology to individual stocks. It is calculated by adjusting the earnings over the past ten years to the current year for inflation and taking the average of the adjusted earnings and dividing the stock price by the average. It smoothes out the commodity price and profit margin fluctuations across the cycle and gives a more real picture of the stock valuation.

P/B is also a relatively better indicator for commodity company stocks when compared with the historical valuations. The reason is, unlike revenue and profit, the book value is relatively stable. In general, commodity prices over the long term are driven by market supply and demand. Commodity producers do not view temporarily low prices or margins as a trigger for conducting impairment tests, which will affect the book value of the company shares.

An example of P/E, P/B, and Shiller P/E for Chevron is shown in Figure 9.13. Chevron's stock cannot be evaluated with regular P/E

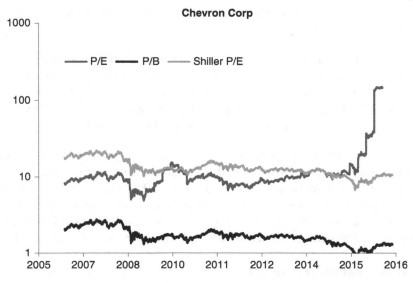

Figure 9.13   CVX P/E, P/B, Shiller P/E

as its earnings are now negative. The ratio went to 150 before that because its earnings declined drastically from 2015. This clearly does not make sense with valuation. P/B and Shiller P/E give a correct measure on the historical valuation of the stock.

A generally better time to buy commodity companies is when the P/B and Shiller P/E ratios are at their lower ends for the recent cycles. The better companies to buy are those that have stronger balance sheets, have higher profit margins, care to reserve enough funds for rainy days, and are traded at lower historical P/B. Very few commodity companies are good for long-term holdings. A better time to sell them is when P/B and Shiller P/E are at the high end of the recent cycle, which is usually also when the commodity prices are at the high end of the cycle.

That was what Buffett did with PetroChina, the giant Chinese oil producer. He bought the stock in 2002 when the oil price was at $20 a barrel and P/B of PetroChina stock was around 1. Then he sold the stock in 2007 when the oil price climbed to above $70 and P/B ratio was at an all-time high of 4. As of September 2016, P/B of PetroChina stock was about 0.7. He had a perfect timing for selling the stock. But then Buffett used some of the profits to buy U.S. oil producer ConocoPhillips in 2008 when the oil price was at an all-time high. This is what he wrote in his 2008 shareholder letter a few months later:

> I bought a large amount of ConocoPhillips stock when oil and gas prices were near their peak. I in no way anticipated the dramatic fall in energy prices that occurred in the last half of the year.... Even if prices should rise, moreover, the terrible timing of my purchase has cost Berkshire several billion dollars.[7]

A more recent example is billionaire activist investor Carl Icahn, who bought into contract driller Transocean in 2013 when the oil price was hovering at around $100 a barrel. The collapse of the oil price idled its rigs, resulting in sharp revenue decline. Carl Icahn lost around 80 percent with this investment and sold out. The commodity market is merciless if you buy at the peaks of the cycles.

Intrinsic Value Calculations

With the intrinsic valuation approach, investors try to reach an absolute valuation of the business and compare the valuation with the stock price. As discussed in Chapter 5, the intrinsic value of a business is equal to the discounted value of the cash flow that can be generated by the business during its remaining life. The cash flow can come from the earnings through the operations of the business; it can also be from the sales of the company's assets. Therefore, the intrinsic value can be estimated based on the earnings power of the company or the net assets that the company owns or the combination of both the earnings power and the assets. Valuation approaches include:

- Net cash
- Net-net working capital (NNWC)
- Net current asset value (NCAV)
- Book value
- Discounted cash flow (earnings)
- Graham Number
- Earnings power value
- Peter Lynch Fair Value
- Median P/S value

The first four, net cash, net-net working capital, net current asset value, and tangible book value, are based purely on the assets of the company. They have been discussed in detail in the deep-value-investing section in Chapter 2. The first three are for the calculation of the fire-sale value of a business's assets and do not consider the business's other assets and earnings power.

Discounted cash flow (earnings) was explained extensively in Chapter 5. I will discuss the other approaches here.

Graham Number

Graham Number is an intrinsic value calculation method named after Benjamin Graham, the father of value investing. It is calculated as follows:

$$\text{Graham Number} = \text{SquareRoot of } (22.5 * \text{Book Value per Share} * \text{Earnings per Share})$$

It can also be calculated as:

$$\text{Graham Number} = \text{SquareRoot of } (22.5 * \text{Net Income} * \text{Common Shareholder's Equity}) / \text{Shares Outstanding}$$

Graham did not actually publish a formula like this. But in *The Intelligent Investor*, regarding the criteria for purchases, he wrote:[8]

> Current price should not be more than 15 times average earnings of the past three years.
>
> Current price should not be more than 1.5 times the book value last reported. However, a multiplier of earnings below 15 could justify a correspondingly higher multiplier of assets. As a rule of thumb, we suggest that the product of the multiplier times the ratio of price to book value should not exceed 22.5. (This figure corresponds to 15 times earnings and 1.5 times book value. It would admit an issue selling at only 9 times earnings and 2.5 times asset value, etc.)

Unlike the valuation methods such as DCF, Graham Number is solely dependent on how the company has done in the latest year. It takes into account both the assets and the earnings power of the company. But it does not consider earnings growth in the valuation.

In general, Graham Number is a very conservative way of evaluating a stock. But because it only looks at the latest earnings and the book value of the company, it does not work well with cyclical companies. It works better with noncyclical manufacturing companies that earn profit by making tangible products. Because it does not take the growth factor into the calculation, it punishes growth companies. It cannot be applied to the companies with negative book values, and it may underestimate the value of asset-light businesses.

Earnings Power Value (EPV)

Earnings power value (EPV) is an intrinsic value calculation methodology developed by Columbia value investing professor Bruce Greenwald, who considers the discounted cash flow model unreliable because it depends heavily on assumptions of future profitability, the cost of capital, and the future growth rate.[9] In the earnings power value approach, he looks for the equivalent asset value of the business from its earnings power. The enterprise value of a company is equal to the normalized earnings divided by the cost of capital. The earnings power value of a company is equal to the enterprise value plus the net assets of the company.

To eliminate the fluctuations caused by business cycles, past profit margins, revenue, and tax rate are averaged over at least one business cycle to arrive at the normalized earnings power. Growth is not considered in this model.

Compared with DCF model, EPV uses mostly existing financial data for the calculation. There is no need to assume the growth rate and the years to grow. But as in any intrinsic value calculation, assumptions are used that may affect the accuracy of the calculation. In the case of EPV, the assumption regarding the cost of capital can drastically affect the results. The estimate of excess depreciation and amortization is also subjective.

If a company is heavily in debt, we may find that its EPV is negative, as in the case of Alliance Data Systems. The company has been able to consistently grow its revenue and earnings. But as of June 2016, it has close to $12 billion in debt. The interest payment on its debt ate almost one-third of its operating income, even in the currently historically low interest rate environment. Because of the heavy debt, its EPV is negative. In the meantime, the company seems to be experiencing shrinking profit margins. Do you still remember the warning signs?

Peter Lynch Fair Value

In Chapter 5, I explained Lynch's rule of thumb of fair P/E: The fair P/E for a growth company is about the same as its earnings growth. This can be used to estimate the fair price of growth companies. We have:

$$\text{Fair P/E} = \text{Earnings Growth Rate}$$

Please note that here we ignore the percentage sign with the growth rate. So, if a company grows at 20 percent a year, we use 20 for earnings growth rate instead of 0.2. Therefore:

$$\text{Peter Lynch Fair Value} = \text{Earnings Growth Rate} * \text{Earnings}$$

Long-term earnings growth rate needs to be used in this calculation. In the growth rate calculation, I prefer to use the growth rate of earnings before interest, tax, and depreciation and amortization. This more accurately reflects the growth of the business operations and is not subject to inaccuracies caused by the estimates of depreciation and amortization or nonrecurring distortions of earnings caused by discontinued operations, tax events, and so forth.

Peter Lynch Fair Value calculation applies well to growing companies that have a growth rate between 15 and 25 percent a year. It tends to underestimate the fair value for slower-growing companies these days, as the interest rate is much lower than it was when Lynch wrote the book.

I want to note that Peter Lynch Fair Value is different from the valuation implied by Peter Lynch's earnings line. In the Peter Lynch earnings line, P/E ratio is always kept at 15; in the fair value calculation, P/E is equal to the growth rate, which can be higher or lower than 15 percent per year.

Median P/S Value

With median P/S value, we assume that the fair valuation of a stock is at the median of its historical price/sales ratio. To smooth out the effect caused by business cycles, we examine the long-term historical price/sale ratio of the stock and find the median value over that period. In GuruFocus's calculation, we use a 10-year period.

Median P/S Value is calculated as:

$$\text{Median P/S Value} = \text{Total Annual Sales} / \text{Shares Outstanding}$$

$$* \text{10-Year Median P/S Ratio}$$

The reason we use the price/sales ratio instead of price/earnings ratio or price/book ratio is because a company's earnings or book value can go into negative territory, and the price/sales ratio is independent of profit margin and can be applied to a broader range of situations. Also, a company's revenue is less sensitive to business cycles than its profit margins and earnings.

As explained in the P/S ratio section, stock prices have historically shown strong correlations with revenue for many companies. For instance, drugmaker Johnson & Johnson's stock price has been fluctuating at about 3.5 times its revenue per share over the past 23 years. For heavy-duty equipment maker Caterpillar, the multiple is about 0.95; for online retailer Amazon, it is about 2.25. This strong correlation can be used to estimate the current fair price for the stock.

Median P/S fair value estimates work well for both steadily performing companies with constant profit margins and cyclical companies whose profit margins fluctuate near a constant level over the long term (e.g., Caterpillar). But if a company's profit margin is on the long-term trend of deviating from its past, this method may overestimate the fair price if the companies are experiencing declining profit margins, or underestimate if the companies are expanding profit margins. For instance, if Amazon expands its profit margin as its more profitable cloud services continue to grow faster than other segments of the company, its stock price may go above the long-term average of 2.25 times revenue per share.

■ ■ ■

Don't be daunted by the myriad ways of evaluating the worth of a business. Once, when I showed the calculations to an investor, he said that he wished there were only one way that would apply to all. Unfortunately, it's not that simple. But it's not that hard, either, if you know what is in the calculations.

When looking at these numbers, think about the underlying business and business performance. Judge whether the business value is dominated by its earnings power or its assets, whether it is growing, and how sustainable its growth is. Then apply the approach that best fits.

If a company has no earnings power and cannot generate positive free cash flow over a full business cycle, it is not a viable business and probably worth, at a maximum, the liquidation value of the assets. If a business generates profit, no rational business owner would sell it at its liquidation value. Its capability of generating cash flow is where the value is.

We can get a taste of these approaches with the valuations on some household names. The values were calculated in September 2016. The discount rate for DCF is 12 percent while for EPV it is 9 percent. The results are shown below:

Company	Price	Book Value	Graham Number	EPV	DCF	Lynch Fair Value	Median P/S Value
Apple Inc.	112	23	65	69	244	171	136
Amazon.com Inc.	829	35	49	30	43	101	508
General Dynamics Corp.	156	36	0	81	101	107	111
Alphabet Inc.	775	180	292	259	709	269	736
Microsoft Corp.	57	9	17	32	24	0	43
Netflix Inc.	97	6	6	9	0	0	44
Wal-Mart Stores Inc.	71	25	45	83	55	0	79
Wells Fargo & Co.	44	35	50	−8	0	0	44

As discussed in the previous section, book value is a reasonable valuation for banks and insurance companies. Among these companies, only Wells Fargo, one of the biggest banks in the United States, is traded not far from its book value. All other companies are traded far above their book values, as they should be. Graham Number and EPV both use the combination of assets and earnings power, and neither takes growth factor into the calculation. They both underestimate the value of fast-growing companies like Apple and Alphabet or asset-light companies like Microsoft. General Dynamics has a negative tangible book value and its Graham Number cannot be calculated.

DCF can only be applied to the companies that will grow consistently into the foreseeable future. Among these companies, Apple, Alphabet, and General Dynamics have demonstrated consistent growth. Apple seems to be undervalued with DCF calculation.

Alphabet, General Dynamics, and Wal-Mart are overvalued with the DCF model.

None of these valuation methods can justify the stock prices of Amazon and Netflix. Even median P/S value, which is based on where the stock was traded in the past, understated where they should be traded.

To further understand these valuation approaches, we can take another look at the prices Buffett paid for three public companies Berkshire Hathaway acquired after 2009. Berkshire acquired Burlington Northern Santa Fe in 2010, Lubrizol in 2012, and Precision Castparts in 2016. The prices Buffett paid and the valuations calculated from different approaches around the times of announcement are included in the table below. If we assume that Buffett paid fair value for the acquisitions, book value, Graham Number, and EPV are too conservative; the stocks of good companies cannot be bought at those prices. DCF calculation and Peter Lynch Fair Value both give quite reasonable estimates of the fair value of these companies, as shown in the table below:

Company	Date	Acquisition Price	Book Value	Graham Number	EPV	DCF	Lynch Fair Value	Median P/S Value
Burlington Northern Santa Fe	Sept., 2009	100	35	68	17	91	103	69
Lubrizol Corp.	Sept., 2011	135	34	65	52	114	142	64
Precision Castparts Corp	Dec., 2015	250	81	31	79	249	169	210

Keep in mind that, before the announcements of the acquisitions, the stocks of these companies were traded roughly 30 to 40 percent lower. That is the margin of safety we should rely on when we look at the stock price relative to the results from the DCF model. If we apply this thinking to the companies in the previous table, none of the stocks offer the margin of safety relative to the DCF model, except Apple.

The table below summarizes the calculation and applications of these intrinsic value calculation methods:

Valuation Methods	Assets	Earnings Power	Combined	Growth Considered	Where to Apply
Net cash	x			No	Fire sale, money-losing companies
Net-net working capital	x			No	
Net current asset value	x			No	
Book value	x			No	Banks, insurance
Discounted cash flow (earnings)		x		Yes	Predictable revenue and earnings
Graham Number			x	No	Asset-heavy companies
Earnings power value			x	No	Asset-heavy companies
Peter Lynch Fair Value		x		Yes	Fast growers
Median P/S value				N/A	Stable average margin over cycles

Rate of Return

Rate of return–based valuation, as suggested by its name, looks at the potential rate of return on the capital that is invested. Though not as popular as valuation ratios or intrinsic value–based valuation, rate of returns gives a straightforward indication of the returns that an investor can expect from this investment.

Rate of return–based valuation focuses on the earnings power of the investment. Its main advantage is that it can be used to compare the returns on alternative investments, such as CDs, money market funds, bonds, or real estate. In principle, investors should always invest in the assets that will generate the highest risk-adjusted returns.

There are two ways to calculate the rate of return with stocks: earnings yield and forward rate of return.

Earnings Yield

Earnings yield is simply the reciprocal of P/E ratio:

$$\text{Earnings Yield} = \text{Earnings/Price}$$

So, if a stock has a P/E ratio of 20, its earnings yield is 1/20 or 5 percent. In this school of thinking, earnings from a business are considered the return to the shareholders. Earnings yield is the rate of return on the price they pay. The return isn't necessarily in cash. It can be in the forms of cash dividends, or share value increase through share buybacks, debt payment, and reinvestments in the business.

Earnings yield is also sometimes calculated as EBIT/EV, that is, the ratio of earnings before interest and tax over enterprise value. In this calculation, it is the reciprocal of EV/EBIT, which is a variation of P/E, as introduced in the P/E ratio section. The advantage of the calculation is that it reflects the true price that investors pay by using enterprise value. The disadvantage is that interest and tax are real expenses to shareholders and the calculation results are only effective for comparisons among companies with similar effective interest rates and tax rates.

In earnings yield calculation, no credit is given to the growth of the company. A company that grows will generate higher returns over time and is more valuable. This factor is considered in the forward rate of return calculation.

Forward Rate of Return

Forward rate of return is a method that Don Yacktman applies in his investment approach.[10] He defines forward rate of return as the normalized free cash flow yield plus real growth plus inflation. He views stocks as bonds, so it makes more sense to value an investment by the potential rate of return, just like with bonds.

Forward rate of return is calculated as:

$$\text{Forward Rate of Return} = \text{Normalized Free Cash Flow / Price}$$
$$+ \text{Growth Rate}$$

Normalized free cash is the average of the free cash flow from the company over the previous market cycle. The growth rate is how fast the free cash flow will grow in the future. A stock has a higher forward rate of return if its price is low or the company's growth rate is high.

■ ■ ■

If we apply the calculations to U.S. retailers, we get:

Company	Earnings Yield (%)	Earnings Yield (EBIT/EV) (%)	Forward Rate of Return (%)
Costco Wholesale Corp.	3.5	5.6	11.5
Dollar General Corp.	6.1	10.4	15.3
Dollar Tree Inc.	3.9	6.0	19.1
Target Corp.	7.8	10.2	6.0
Wal-Mart Stores Inc.	6.5	9.0	7.8

With all three calculations, Dollar General seems more promising than the others because of its higher earnings yield and higher forward rate of return.

Both earnings yield and forward rate of return calculations can also be applied to the overall stock market. The results can be used to compare it with the returns on CDs, money market funds, and bonds. An equity risk premium over risk-free rate from short-term government bonds is usually required by investors because of the volatility and uncertainty of stock investments. This is also how the interest rate affects the attractiveness of the stock market from the aspect of the potential rate of return. I will discuss market valuation in detail in the next chapter.

■ ■ ■

As I conclude this chapter, I want to point out that investors should not be obsessed with the valuation calculations. All calculations involve assumptions. They are valid only if the underlying businesses perform as expected. Over the long term, investment return is more a function of business performance than the valuation, unless the valuation goes extreme. More effort should be put into identifying good businesses and buying them at reasonable valuations.

CHAPTER 10

Market Cycles and Valuations

Since starting GuruFocus, I have often been asked by friends or users what the stock market will do this week, this month, or this year. I wish I had a better answer than J. P. Morgan's "It will fluctuate."

To value investors, there is no stock market. There is just a market of stocks in which investors can trade. Stock market moves are the collective movements of individual stocks. Yet, many players are guided by what others do in the market, and their movements form a tide resembling a stock market. Also, as more investors trade market index ETFs and care little about the individual stocks within the ETFs, the stocks tend to move together in one direction. That is probably the stock market that people talk about.

Though I don't know where the market will go in the short term, I have learned a few things about the stock market that I consider important even for value investors who don't pay too much attention to the overall market: (1) over the long term, the stock market always goes up; (2) the stock market has cycles; and (3) higher current market valuation results in lower returns in the future and vice versa. Having a good understanding of these principles can be useful during extreme times.

Over the Long Term, the Market Will Always Go Up

Over the long term, the stock market as a whole always goes up. This seems obvious. But investors tend to forget it when things get scary; it is during these tough times that investors most need conviction and optimism. The direction of the stock market is nothing but ups and downs of the total market value of the companies that supply us with what we need in life, directly or indirectly. Over time, these companies will produce more products and provide more services due to the growth of the population and the improvement of living standards. The average prices of their products will go up due to inflation. The overall revenue and profit will increase, and they will be worth more over time.

At times, the market value has gone down, sometimes by a lot, or has hovered around certain levels for a long while. Market crashes can be painful. The media make it sound like the world will end and everything will go to zero. But if we look back, every one of these crashes posed opportunities to put money in stocks for great returns. Undoubtedly, the market will crash again, but over the long term, humans will consume more products and services than they do today. The economy will generate more profit and become more valuable. Investment return is inversely proportional to the price you pay. The lower the price you pay, the higher return you get. A stock market crash is nothing but a time when others are willing to sell their shares that will be worth more on the cheap, presenting you with opportunities for hefty returns. Buying when the mass is selling makes a significant difference on your investment returns.

That is how Baron Rothschild made his fortune in the eighteenth century. He famously said: "Buy when there's blood in the streets, even if the blood is your own." Sir John Templeton made a killing by buying 100 shares of each NYSE-listed company that was selling for less than a dollar during the Great Depression.

Both Templeton and Warren Buffett predicted that by the end of the century, the Dow Jones Industrial Average will be above 1,000,000. Currently, the index is around 20,000; 1,000,000 seems like an astronomical number, but it takes an average gain of only 4.8 percent per year for the Dow to reach that level by the year 2100, which is far below the average gain of the Index over the past century.

Of course, most of the people who read this book will not be around by the year 2100. As John Keynes said, "In the long run we are all dead." But all of us will be able to ride part of the trend to the Dow reaching 1,000,000. Over the long term, the market always goes up. Though maybe simple and obvious, this is extremely important to remember when you feel the need to act from fear.

It Will Be Cyclical

Though the market will assuredly be higher in the future, the ride won't be smooth. It will always go through cycles of extreme roller-coaster ups and downs, except this ride will end at gradually higher levels. People tend to forget that the sun will come out again during times that seem endlessly dark; they also forget that bright daylight doesn't last forever during good times. It is cyclical.

Howard Marks likens the stock market to a pendulum that swings between the extremes of euphoria and depression, or overpriced and undervalued.[1] Just like a physical pendulum, the market spends the least amount of time in the middle. Since the end of World War II, there have been ten bear markets—defined as declines of 20 percent or more in the S&P 500 Index. Additionally, the market has had 24 corrections—defined as declines of 10 percent or more in the S&P 500 Index. It has gone through just as many bull markets, with periods during which the S&P 500 doubled without correction.

The main reason the stock market is cyclical is that the underlying economy is cyclical, driven by human behavior. Figure 10.1 shows the S&P 500 Index, the historical U.S. corporate after-tax

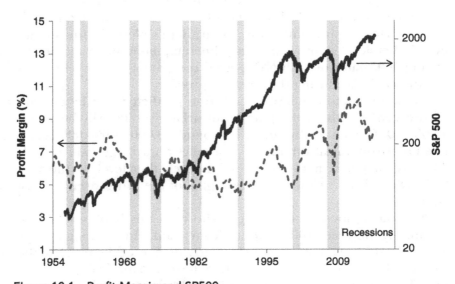

Figure 10.1   Profit Margin and SP500
Source: Downloaded from http://www.GuruFocus.com on 10/3/2016

profit margins, and recession periods since World War II. Clearly, the profit margins of U.S. corporations are cyclical. The corporations continue to go through the cycles of margin expansion and compression. The periods of margin compressions are usually associated with economic recessions, which typically lead to market declines. Since World War II, the U.S. economy has gone through 11 recessions, and almost every one of them triggered a bear market. During recessions, profit margin shrinks, earnings are poor, weak companies go bankrupt, and even many stronger ones must cut the number of employees to justify fallen sales and profits. News is bad, and investors are in poor economic shape, pessimistic, and in no mood for buying. The stock market tanks.

Then it always recovers. During recessions and bear markets, valuations are low and less capital is there to compete for the ample investment opportunities now available. The potential returns from these investments become higher. The investors who focus on value will recognize the opportunities and start investing. They are followed by a few other brave ones, then by the large crowds who watched the success of the earlier investors and now consider it safe to invest. The price continues to climb and more capital floods in to chase returns. As the price goes up, the potential returns diminish. Risk becomes undervalued. But momentum will continue until the crowds discover that their investments suffer unexpected losses. Then the downcycle begins. The cycle repeats over and over again.

As investors, we must remember the inevitability of cyclicity and keep abreast of where we are in the cycle. When the market was going up and investment returns were rosy, the market valuation may have been pushed to overvalued levels. Overvaluation with the stock market usually comes with excess capital investment and overcapacity in businesses. Stock prices are sensitive to bad news when the valuation is high. Bad news in business will trigger the market downturn. The valuation will revert to the mean, and the pendulum will swing in the other direction.

The dashed line in the chart in Figure 10.1, corporate profit margin, is a good indicator of where we are in the current economic cycle, which started in 2009. We have seen the peak of above 10 percent in profit margin from 2011 through 2013. It stands at around 8 percent as of October 2016 and in the downtrend direction.

Market Valuations

Another important parameter to observe is the overall market valuation. As with individual stocks, the overall market can be measured with P/E ratio and P/S ratio. But just like with cyclical companies, the whole economy is cyclical. During recessions, profit margins are low and earnings are depressed. P/E ratio gives a false indication of the market valuation. Yale professor Robert Shiller's cyclically adjusted P/E is a better indicator for the market valuation. Daily updated Shiller P/E can be found on GuruFocus.com by using this link: http://www.gurufocus.com/shiller-PE.php.

The historical mean of Shiller P/E is 16.7. As of February 2017, the ratio is at 28.6, which is about 71 percent higher than the historical mean. Where it stands now is about the same as in the fall of 2007, just before the unfolding of the financial crisis. Throughout history, Shiller P/E ratio was higher than it is now only at the peak before the Great Depression and during the dot-com bubble. Over the past two decades, Shiller P/E was never lower than the historical mean except at the time of the market crash of 2009.

The ratio that Buffett uses for measuring the market valuation is to look at the P/S ratio of the overall market. Here the price is the total of market values of all the companies in the United States, and sales are Gross National Product (GNP) of the United States. Therefore, it is the ratio of the total market value over GNP. Buffett calls this ratio "probably the best single measure of where valuations stand at any given moment."[2]

Because this is a P/S ratio, it does not give a direct indication of whether the market is expensive or cheap. But it can be compared with historical values. Also, the revert-to-mean calculation can be used to forecast the future returns of the overall market.

In the calculation on GuruFocus.com,[3] we use Gross Domestic Product (GDP) instead of GNP for sales because GDP data is updated faster. Though the two numbers have different meanings, they both measure the production levels in an economy, and their differences in numbers have been minimal. For the total market value, we use "Wilshire 5000 Full Cap Price Index" instead of the total market values of all U.S. companies, which includes all public and private companies. The reason is because we can get daily values for Wilshire 5000 Full Cap Price Index, whereas the total market values of all U.S. companies are updated quarterly. Our calculation gives different absolute values from the total market value over GNP calculation, but when compared with its own historical values, this ratio should give a similar picture and conclusion if the total market cap of all U.S. companies is used.

Figure 10.2 shows the ratio of total market cap over GDP since 1971. We can see that during the past four decades, this ratio has varied within a very wide range. The lowest point was about 35 percent in the previous deep recession of 1982, while the highest point was 148 percent during the tech bubble in 2000. The market went from extremely undervalued in 1982 to extremely overvalued in 2000. The historical mean is 78 percent. As of October 2016, the ratio stands at above 120 percent, which is about 55 percent higher than the historical mean. It is higher than it was before the market crash in 2007. Only the year 2000 peak was higher.

Both Shiller P/E and the ratio of total-market-value/GDP suggest that the market is significantly overvalued as of February 2017. But the tricky part is the interest rate. The interest rate has never been this low; if it continues to stay this low, the market may not be as overvalued as it seems.

Both the trend of profit margins and market valuations suggest that we are currently at the late stage of this cycle, though this does not tell us when the downturn is coming. At this stage of the

Figure 10.2   TMC/GDP

cycle, investors need to act very cautiously and be financially and psychologically prepared for a possible downturn. Also, don't forget to update your watch list!

Projected Future Market Returns

Though the market valuation does not tell us when the downturn is coming or where the stock market will go in the short term, it does tell us a lot about the future market returns we can expect. Its track record is quite satisfactory.

The future returns of the entire stock market are determined by the following three factors:

1. *Business growth*

If we look at a particular business, the value of the business is determined by how much money this business can make. The growth in the value of the business comes from the growth of the earnings of the business. This growth in the business value is reflected as the price appreciation of the company stock if the market recognizes the value, which it always does, eventually. If we look at the overall economy, the growth in the value of the entire stock market comes from the growth of corporate earnings. Over the long term, overall corporate earnings grow as fast as the economy itself.

2. *Dividends*

Dividends are an important portion of the investment return. Dividends come from the cash earning of a business. Everything equal, a higher dividend payout ratio, in principle, should result in a lower growth rate. Therefore, if a company pays out dividends while still growing earnings, the dividend is an additional return for the shareholders besides the appreciation of the business value.

3. *Change in the market valuation*

Although the value of a business does not change overnight, its stock price often does. Over the long run, stock market valuation reverts to its mean, regardless whether it is measured by P/E, P/S, P/B, and so on. A higher current valuation certainly correlates with lower long-term future returns. Conversely, a lower current valuation level correlates with a higher future return.

So, what return is the market likely to deliver from its current level? Putting together the contributions from all three factors, the return of an investment can be estimated by the following formula:

Investment Return (%) = Dividend Yield (%) + Business Growth (%)

+ Change of Valuation (%)

The first two items of the equation are straightforward. The third can be calculated if we know the beginning and ending market ratios of the time period (T) considered. If we assume the beginning ratio is Rb and the ending ratio is Re, then the contribution in the change of the valuation can be calculated from this:

$$(Re/Rb)^{1/T} - 1$$

The investment return is thus equal to:

Investment Return (%) = Dividend Yield (%) + Business Growth (%)

$$+ (Re/Rb)^{1/T} - 1$$

From this equation, we can calculate the likely returns that the stock market will generate from the current valuation level Rb. In the calculation, the time period T we used was eight years, which is about the length of a full economic cycle. By using eight years, we assume that the market valuation will revert to its historical mean (Re) in a full market cycle. This mean is about 78 percent if we use the total market cap over GDP for the overall market valuation ratio.

The projected expected return is reflected in Figure 10.3. To verify this model, the historical actual return is also shown. The actual return is calculated with the actual data of Wilshire 5000 Full Cap Price Index. To get the actual return for the year 1990, for example, we calculate the compound annualized return of Wilshire 5000 Full Cap Price Index from 1990 through 1998. The actual return data can only be calculated up to 2008 at this point because 2016 Wilshire 5000 Full Cap Price Index is the latest data available.

We can see that the calculations largely predicted the trend in the returns of the stock market. For the 1970s and early 1980s, the calculated returns were higher than the actual market returns. For the late 1980s and 1990s, the calculated returns were lower. The discrepancy may be caused by the swing in interest rates. The interest rate was going up quickly in the 1970s and the stock market faced a headwind. As interest rates went down in the 1980s, the stock market was riding the tailwind and delivered higher-than-expected returns.

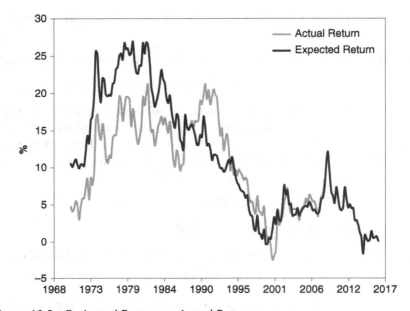

Figure 10.3   Projected Return vs. Actual Return
Source: Downloaded from http://www.GuruFocus.com on 10/7/2016

Starting in the mid-1990s, the long-term interest rate as measured by the ten-year yield went below 6 percent. The actual return followed the projected return very closely.

As of February 2017, the calculation shows that the stock market is likely to return −0.5 percent per year, including dividends, in the next eight years. This paints a very pale picture for future market returns. Only at the peak of the tech bubble in 2000 was the projected return this low.

It is possible that the calculation is too conservative, as I assume the valuation ratio will revert to its mean at 78 percent since 1970, although the comparison between the actual return and the projected return does not indicate so. If interest continues to stay this low, the valuation ratio may continue to stay at higher levels. If the ratio of the total market value over GDP is at its current level of 120 percent in eight years, the expected return is a much higher 5 percent a year. If the ratio is midway between the historical mean and what it is now, the projected return is a little above 2 percent, which implies a flat market in the next eight years if the dividend contribution is subtracted from the calculation.

But this doesn't mean there won't be opportunities in the stock market. The stock market will continue to cycle, as it always has. It is probably close to one extreme right now. It may swing to the other extreme quicker than average investors are prepared for. In the meantime, it will create tremendous opportunities for those who understand cycles and are well prepared. In the peak of the dot-com bubble in 2000, the calculated expected return was close to nothing, which it did deliver in the following decade. But over those ten years, the economy and the market went through two downcycles. The far-lower valuation caused by these downcycles lifted the projected return to considerably higher levels, which the market again delivered in the years that followed. It is certain that the market will go through more downcycles in the next decade. Cycles never stop. There will be times when the market again positions itself for much higher returns.

Naturally, far fewer people are interested in buying stocks as the stock market crashes. The news is bad and the downtrend may continue, although the valuation is now more appealing and the projected return is higher. If you are tempted and need a little more conviction, take a look at what the insiders are doing.

Insider Trends

As a group, company insiders such as corporate executives and those on the board of directors act much more rationally during market crashes. This may not be surprising; they are more business savvy and are better able to use public information to analyze businesses. More importantly, they are now dealing with their own money. An earlier study found that insiders are mostly value investors. They are net buyers of relatively low P/E stocks and net sellers of relatively high P/E stocks, and they tend to sell more when market valuation is high and buy more during market selloffs. Immediately after Black Monday on October 19, 1987, when the Dow lost 22.6 percent, insiders were heavy buyers (90% being buyers). October 20, 1987, had more insiders buying than any other day during the study period from 1975 to 1989.[4] Given the insiders' knowledge of their companies, this buying suggests that the collapse was an irrational reaction to the stock price declines over the previous two weeks. Insiders acted quickly and grasped the opportunity.

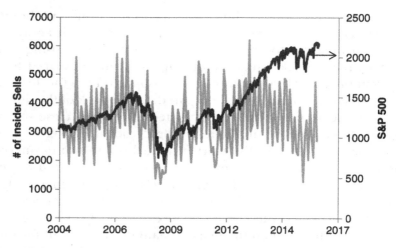

Figure 10.4   Insider Sales

The data over the past decade demonstrates that the behavior of insiders has not changed from 30 years ago. Insiders don't join the crowd in market selloffs. Figure 10.4 shows the aggregated monthly number of total insider sales since 2004. Only the open market sells of insiders are counted. No weight was given in the data to the numbers of shares sold or the dollar amount.

The S&P 500 Index is also shown in the chart for comparison purposes. Interestingly, the envelope of insider sells chart has a very similar shape to the S&P 500 Index. Insiders sold the most at the market high of 2007. They sold the least at the market lows during the worst period of the financial crisis from September 2008 to April 2009, the U.S. government shutdown threat in August 2011, and the market correction from late 2015 to early 2016.

Not only do insiders tend not to sell at the market lows, they also buy more as the market declines, just the opposite of what the broad market does. Figure 10.5 shows the monthly number of open market insider buys from 2004. The buying activities picked up as the market started to decline in late 2007 and reached a peak exactly when they sold the least during the financial crisis. Similar behavior was observed during the crisis of the U.S. government shutdown in 2011 and the correction from late 2015 to early 2016.

This clearly illustrates that when the market panicked and was selling indiscriminately, insiders as a whole were doing exactly the opposite. They remained confident regarding their companies and

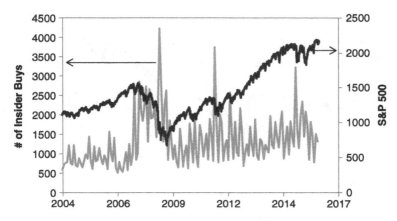

Figure 10.5   Insider Buys
Data source: S&P500 and Wilshire 5000

purchased many more shares than they normally did. These purchases were rewarded greatly in the years that followed.

When we draw the ratio of the aggregated monthly number of insider buys over insider sells, we get Figure 10.6. Much of the time, the ratio stays at less than 0.5, which means that insider buying activities are less than 50 percent of selling activities. However, as the market declined, the ratio picked up in 2008; by October 2008, it was at 1; it peaked in November 2008 at 2.4; and it peaked again at 1.9 in March 2009 when the stock market hit bottom. Two other peaks were observed in August 2011 and August 2015 through January 2016. Every one of the peaks happened after the market declined considerably. The higher the decline was, the more buys the insiders made.

This data shows that insiders as a group acted rationally during market crashes. Their aggregated buying/selling activities ratio can serve as another good indicator of the attractiveness of the stock valuation during downcycles.

By the way, all the data mentioned in this chapter, market valuations, the projected returns, and insider activity ratios are available on GuruFocus.com and are updated daily.

■ ■ ■

Understanding the economic cycles and market valuation will not help anyone predict the direction of the market in the short term or even in midterms like a year or two. But it keeps investors

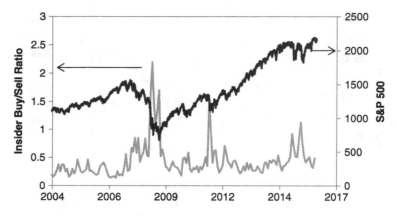

Figure 10.6   Insider Buy/Sell Ratio
Data source: S&P500 and Wilshire 5000

from looking in the rearview mirror. They will have a clearer view of the future and be able to stay rational when the market gets euphoric or sinks into fear again.

For analyzing individual companies, having a good knowledge of business cycles and the likely future market returns can be useful in evaluating management's capital allocation decisions, their aggressiveness in accounting, and the quality of earnings related to pension-fund return assumptions.

Buffett calls himself a bottom-up value investor and rarely talks about the general market. But he has a tremendous understanding of business cycles, the role of interest rates, market valuations, and the likely future returns and risks. A good book to read about this topic is Marks's *The Most Important Thing,* [5] which I strongly recommend.

Over the long term, we should always be optimistic. At the current late stage of the business cycle, investors should stay defensive and be prepared for the next downcycle. They should focus their investments on the quality companies that not only can pass the test of bad times, but also can come out stronger.

Now, more than any other time in the past decade, it is vital to invest only in good companies.

Epilogue

Over the years, I have made plenty of mistakes with stocks and lost money on many of them, even after I read Peter Lynch and Warren Buffett. The mistake that scared me the most was when I bought into Sears at $170 in 2007, thinking it was extremely undervalued. Then a few months later, I suddenly recognized that Sears is a poor retailer and my wife never went to Sears to buy anything. I sold it at about the same price. Although I didn't lose money on Sears, I still get nightmares from it today. When I was writing Chapter 2 three months ago, the stock was traded at above $14. Now it is below $7. This made me think more about the quality of business and built my conviction of never buying low-quality companies again, no matter how undervalued they seem to be!

Then I made mistakes with good companies. I didn't hold them long enough and missed further gains with great companies like Starbucks and Danaher.

I did do it right with companies like Berkshire Hathaway, Church & Dwight, EBIX, AutoZone, and a few others.

I put what I learned into GuruFocus value screeners, charts, data, and other research tools over the past 12 years. I wrote this book to share my lessons. I hope that even people who don't analyze stocks full time can benefit from it. I hope that my children can stay in the right framework for investing. I do advise them to take accounting courses in college.

Finally, I want to pull the main ideas together:

1. The risk with buying poorly performing companies is the permanent loss of capital, though the price may look cheap.
2. Good companies are those that are consistently profitable with double-digit operating margins, have double-digit return on invested capital, and are growing at double-digit rates.
3. Buy only good companies and buy them at reasonable prices.

4. Beware of value traps.
5. Don't forget cycles.

If there is one point that you should get from this book, it is, "Buy only good companies!" Stick with good companies, buy them at reasonable prices, and keep learning. You can indeed invest like a Guru.

Notes

Introduction

1. Peter Lynch with John Rothschild, *Beating the Street*, Simon & Schuster paperbacks, New York, 1993
2. John Kenneth Galbraith, *A Short History of Financial Euphoria*, Penguin Books, 1990
3. John O'Farrell, *An Utterly Impartial History of Britain—Or 2000 Years of Upper Class Idiots in Charge*, Doubleday, 2007
4. Warren Buffett, Berkshire Hathaway shareholder letter, 2007, http://www.berkshirehathaway.com/letters/2007ltr.pdf
5. Andrew Bary, "What's Wrong, Warren?" Barron's, 1999, http://www.barrons.com/articles/SB945992010127068546
6. Steven Romick, "Don't Be Surprised—Speech to CFA Society of Chicago," June 2015, http://www.fpafunds.com/docs/special-commentaries/cfa-society-of-chicago-june-2015-final1.pdf?sfvrsn=2
7. Peter Lynch with John Rothschild, *One Up on Wall Street*, Simon & Schuster paperbacks, New York, 1998

Chapter 1

1. Charlie Munger, USC Law Commencement Speech, 2007, https://www.youtube.com/watch?v=u8ll7rM2yl8
2. Peter Lynch with John Rothschild, *Beating the Street*, Simon & Schuster paperbacks, New York, 1993
3. Peter Lynch with John Rothschild, *One Up on Wall Street*, Simon & Schuster paperbacks, New York, 1998
4. Ibid
5. Oplink Communications, 10K, 2001, https://www.sec.gov/Archives/edgar/data/1022225/000101287001502073/d10k.txt
6. Peter Lynch with John Rothschild, *One Up on Wall Street*, Simon & Schuster paperbacks, New York, 1998
7. "Track Companies, Not Markets [Final Edition]," *USA Today*, p. 04.B, McLean, Virginia, March 7, 1989
8. Peter Lynch with John Rothschild, *One Up on Wall Street*, Simon & Schuster paperbacks, New York, 1998

9. Warren Buffett, Berkshire Hathaway shareholder letter, 1989, http://www.berkshirehathaway.com/letters/1989.html

10. Warren Buffett, *The Commercial and Financial Chronicle*, Dec. 6, 1961

11. Ibid

12. Warren Buffett, Berkshire Hathaway shareholder letter, 1992, http://www.berkshirehathaway.com/letters/1992.html

13. Warren Buffett, Berkshire Hathaway shareholder letter, 2010, http://www.berkshirehathaway.com/letters/2010ltr.pdf

14. Warren Buffett, Berkshire Hathaway shareholder letter, 1993, http://www.berkshirehathaway.com/letters/1993.html

15. Warren Buffett, Berkshire Hathaway shareholder letter, 2006, http://www.berkshirehathaway.com/letters/2006ltr.pdf

16. John Kenneth Galbraith, *A Short History of Financial Euphoria*, Penguin Books, 1990

17. Warren Buffett, Berkshire Hathaway shareholder letter, 1998, http://www.berkshirehathaway.com/letters/1998.html

18. Warren Buffett, Berkshire Hathaway shareholder letter, 2014, http://www.berkshirehathaway.com/letters/2014ltr.pdf

19. Warren Buffett, Berkshire Hathaway shareholder letter, 2012, http://www.berkshirehathaway.com/letters/2012ltr.pdf

20. Warren Buffett, "The Superinvestors of Graham-and-Doddsville," 1984, http://www8.gsb.columbia.edu/alumni/news/superinvestors

21. Peter Lynch with John Rothschild, *One Up on Wall Street*, Simon & Schuster paperbacks, New York, 1998

22. Morgan Housel, "The Peculiar Habits of Successful People," *USA Today*, August 24, 2014, http://www.usatoday.com/story/money/personalfinance/2014/08/24/peculiar-habits-of-successful-people/14447531/

23. Steve Jordon, "Investors Earn Handsome Paychecks by Handling Buffett's Business," *Omaha World-Herald*, April 28, 2013, http://www.omaha.com/money/investors-earn-handsome-paychecks-by-handling-buffett-s-business/article_bb1fc40f-e6f9-549d-be2f-be1ef4c0da03.html

24. Charlie Munger, USC Law Commencement Speech, https://www.youtube.com/watch?v=u8l17rM2yl8

Chapter 2

1. http://www.raiseyourmind.com/motivational/dont-let-the-tall-weeds-cast-a-shadow-on-the-beautiful-flowers-in-your-garden/

2. Benjamin Graham, *The Intelligent Investor*, Harper Collins, 2009

3. Warren Buffett, Berkshire Hathaway shareholder letter, 1993, http://www.berkshirehathaway.com/letters/1993.html

4. Ibid
5. Benjamin Graham, *The Intelligent Investor*, Harper Collins, 2009
6. http://www.gurufocus.com/screener/
7. http://www.gurufocus.com/grahamncav.php
8. Benjamin Graham, *The Intelligent Investor*, Harper Collins, 2009
9. John Kenneth Galbraith, *A Short History of Financial Euphoria*, Penguin Books, 1990
10. Warren Buffett, Berkshire Hathaway shareholder letter, 1989, http://www.berkshirehathaway.com/letters/1989.html
11. Warren Buffett, Berkshire Hathaway shareholder letter, 1992, http://www.berkshirehathaway.com/letters/1992.html
12. Ibid
13. Charlie Munger, USC Law Commencement Speech, https://www.youtube.com/watch?v=u8l17rM2yl8
14. Warren Buffett, Berkshire Hathaway shareholder letter, 1985, http://www.berkshirehathaway.com/letters/1985.html
15. Fairholme Fund Annual Shareholder Letter, 2013, https://static1.squarespace.com/static/53962eb7e4b053c664d74f3d/t/5429b689e4b06a1d711a373a/1412019849559/FAIRX_11.30.13%2Bv2.1WEB_0.pdf
16. Fairholme Fund Semiannual Shareholder Letter, 2016, http://www.fairholmefundsinc.com/Letters/Funds2016SemiAnnualLetter.pdf
17. Warren Buffett, Berkshire Hathaway shareholder letter, 1989, http://www.berkshirehathaway.com/letters/1989.html

Chapter 3

1. Peter Lynch with John Rothschild, *Beating the Street*, Simon & Schuster paperbacks, New York, 1993
2. Warren Buffett, Berkshire Hathaway shareholder letter, 1987, http://www.berkshirehathaway.com/letters/1987.html
3. Warren Buffett, Berkshire Hathaway shareholder letter, 1987, http://www.berkshirehathaway.com/letters/1987.html
4. Ibid
5. Ibid
6. *USA Today*, "Track Companies, Not Markets [Final Edition]," p. 04.B, March 7, 1989, McLean, Virginia
7. Warren Buffett, Berkshire Hathaway shareholder letter, 1985, http://www.berkshirehathaway.com/letters/1985.html
8. Charlie Munger, USC Law Commencement Speech, https://www.youtube.com/watch?v=u8l17rM2yl8

Chapter 4

1. Charlie Munger: *Poor Charlie's Almanack: The Wit and Wisdom of Charles T. Munger*, Donning Company, 2005
2. Peter Lynch with John Rothschild, *One Up on Wall Street*, Simon & Schuster paperbacks, New York, 1998
3. Fairholme Fund Semiannual Shareholder Letter, 2016, http://www.fairholmefundsinc.com/Letters/Funds2016SemiAnnualLetter.pdf
4. Peter Lynch with John Rothschild, *One Up on Wall Street*, Simon & Schuster paperbacks, New York, 1998
5. Warren Buffett, Berkshire Hathaway shareholder letter, 1979, http://www.berkshirehathaway.com/letters/1979.html
6. Warren Buffett, Berkshire Hathaway shareholder letter, 1980, http://www.berkshirehathaway.com/letters/1980.html
7. Warren Buffett, Berkshire Hathaway shareholder letter, 1980, http://www.berkshirehathaway.com/letters/1980.html
8. Howard Marks, *The Most Important Thing: Uncommon Sense for the Thoughtful Investor*, Columbia Business School Publishing, 2013
9. Warren Buffett, Berkshire Hathaway shareholder letter, 1990, http://www.berkshirehathaway.com/letters/1990.html
10. Warren Buffett, Berkshire Hathaway shareholder letter, 1990, http://www.berkshirehathaway.com/letters/1990.html
11. http://www.gurufocus.com/news/394902/seeking-wisdom-from-charlie-munger
12. Warren Buffett, Berkshire Hathaway shareholder letter, 1995, http://www.berkshirehathaway.com/letters/1995.html
13. Warren Buffett, Berkshire Hathaway shareholder letter, 1992, http://www.berkshirehathaway.com/letters/1992.html

Chapter 5

1. Warren Buffett, Berkshire Hathaway shareholder letter, 2004, http://www.berkshirehathaway.com/letters/2004ltr.pdf
2. John Burr Williams, *The Theory of Investment Value*, Fraser Publishing, 1956
3. Berkshire Hathaway shareholder letters, 1972–1999, http://www.berkshirehathaway.com/letters/
4. Warren Buffett, Berkshire Hathaway shareholder letter, 2014, http://www.berkshirehathaway.com/letters/2014ltr.pdf
5. Peter Lynch with John Rothschild, *One Up on Wall Street*, Simon & Schuster paperbacks, New York, 1998

6. Howard Marks, "Economy Reality," 2016, https://www.oaktreecapital
   .com/docs/default-source/memos/economic-reality.pdf
7. Ibid
8. Charlie Munger, *Poor Charlie's Almanack: The Wit and Wisdom of Charles T. Munger*, Donning Company, 2005
9. GuruFocus, "Lauren Templeton: Methods Sir John Templeton Used to Take Advantage of Crisis Events," http://www.gurufocus.com/news/174804/lauren-templeton-methods-sir-john-templeton-used-to-take-advantage-of-crisis-events
10. Warren Buffett, Berkshire Hathaway shareholder letter, 1998, http://www.berkshirehathaway.com/letters/1998.html

Chapter 6

1. Atul Gawande, *The Checklist Manifesto: How to Get Things Right*, Henry Holt and Company, 2009
2. Chesley Sullenberger, Jeffrey Zaslow, *Highest Duty: My Search for What Really Matters*, William Morrow, 2009
3. Walter Schloss: 16 Golden Rules for Investing; http://www.gurufocus.com/news/72536/walter-schloss-16-golden-rules-for-investing
4. Philip A. Fisher, *Common Stocks and Uncommon Profits*, John Wiley & Sons, New York, 1958
5. Peter Lynch with John Rothschild, *One Up on Wall Street*, Simon & Schuster paperbacks, New York, 1998
6. James Montier, *Mind Matters: Joining the Dark Side: Pirates, Spies and Short Sellers*, http://www.designs.valueinvestorinsight.com/bonus/bonuscontent/docs/Montier-Shorting.pdf
7. Warren Buffett, Berkshire Hathaway shareholder letter, 1986, http://www.berkshirehathaway.com/letters/1986.html
8. E. Altman, "Financial Ratios, Discriminant Analysis and the Prediction of Corporate Bankruptcy," *Journal of Finance*, September 1968
9. Joseph D. Piotroski, "Value Investing: The Use of Historical Financial Statement Information to Separate Winners from Losers" (PDF), The University of Chicago Graduate School of Business, January 2002
10. Messod D. Beneish, "The Detection of Earnings Manipulation," http://citeseerx.ist.psu.edu/viewdoc/download?doi=10.1.1.195.3676&rep=rep1&type=pdf
11. Richard G. Sloan, "Do Stock Prices Fully Reflect Information in Accruals and Cash Flows about Future Earnings?" *Accounting Review*, Vol. 71, No. 3 (July 1996), pp. 289–315

12. Owen A. Lamont, Jeremy C. Stein, "Aggregate Short Interest and Market Valuations," *American Economic Review*, May 2004
13. H. Nejat Seyhun et al., "Overreaction or Fundamentals: Some Lessons from Insiders' Response to the Market Crash of 1987," *Journal of Finance*, Vol. 45, No. 5 (February 1990), pp. 1363–1388
14. Charlie Munger, USC Law Commencement Speech, https://www.youtube.com/watch?v=u8117rM2yl8

Chapter 7

1. John Huber, "A 1977 Warren Buffett Interview from the WSJ Archives," http://www.gurufocus.com/news/438345
2. Warren Buffett, Berkshire Hathaway shareholder letter, 2004, http://www.berkshirehathaway.com/letters/2004ltr.pdf
3. Scott Fearson, *Dead Companies Walking*, Macmillan, 2015
4. Peter Lynch with John Rothschild, *One Up on Wall Street*, Simon & Schuster paperbacks, New York, 1998
5. Warren Buffett, Berkshire Hathaway shareholder letter, 2014, http://www.berkshirehathaway.com/letters/2014ltr.pdf
6. Prem Watsa, Fairfax Financial Holdings shareholder letter, 2012, http://s1.q4cdn.com/579586326/files/Letter%20to%20Shareholders%20from%20Annual%20Report%202012%20FINAL_v001_o7033s.pdf
7. https://en.wikipedia.org/wiki/John_S._Chen
8. BlackBerry Financial Data, http://www.gurufocus.com/financials/BBRY
9. Adam Lashinsky, "Amazon's Jeff Bezos: The Ultimate Disrupter," http://fortune.com/2012/11/16/amazons-jeff-bezos-the-ultimate-disrupter/

Chapter 8

1. Bob Isbitts, "Index Funds Beat Active 90% of the Time, Really?" http://www.marketwatch.com/story/index-funds-beat-active-90-of-the-time-really-2014-08-01
2. Warren Buffett, Berkshire Hathaway shareholder letter, 1993, http://www.berkshirehathaway.com/letters/1993.html
3. Joel Greenblatt, *The Little Book That Beats the Market*, John Wiley & Sons, 2010
4. Berkshire Hathaway shareholder letters, 1972–1999, http://www.berkshirehathaway.com/letters/
5. Warren Buffett, Berkshire Hathaway shareholder letter, 1988, http://www.berkshirehathaway.com/letters/1988.html

6. Virginia Reynolds Parker, *Managing Hedge Fund Risk: Strategies and Insights from Investors, Counterparties, Hedge Funds and Regulators*, Risk Books, 2005
7. Ibid

Chapter 9

1. Peter Lynch with John Rothschild, *One Up on Wall Street*, Simon & Schuster paperbacks, New York, 1998
2. Ibid
3. Ibid
4. Ibid
5. Jack Hough, "U.S. Steel Could Rise 50% in a Year," *Barron's*, October 17, 2016
6. Robert Shiller, http://www.econ.yale.edu/~shiller/data.htm
7. Warren Buffett, Berkshire Hathaway shareholder letter, 2008, http://www.berkshirehathaway.com/letters/2008ltr.pdf
8. Benjamin Graham, *The Intelligent Investor*, Harper Collins, 2009
9. Bruce Greenwald, *Value Investing: From Graham to Buffett and Beyond*, John Wiley & Sons, 2004
10. GuruFocus, "Investing Great: Donald Yacktman Answers GuruFocus Readers' Questions," http://www.gurufocus.com/news/171597

Chapter 10

1. Howard Marks, *The Most Important Thing: Uncommon Sense for the Thoughtful Investor*, Columbia Business School Publishing, 2013
2. Warren Buffett and Carol Loomis, "Warren Buffett on the Stock Market," *Fortune*, 2001. http://archive.fortune.com/magazines/fortune/fortune_archive/2001/12/10/314691/index.htm
3. GuruFocus, "Where Are We with Market Valuations?" http://www.gurufocus.com/stock-market-valuations.php
4. H. Nejat Seyhun et al., "Overreaction or Fundamentals: Some Lessons from Insiders' Response to the Market Crash of 1987," *Journal of Finance*, Vol. 45, No. 5 (February 1990), pp. 1363–1388
5. Howard Marks, *The Most Important Thing: Uncommon Sense for the Thoughtful Investor*, Columbia Business School Publishing, 2013

About the Author

Charlie Tian, PhD, is the founder and CEO of the value-investing website GuruFocus.com. He is the creator of the website's value screeners, strategies, and research tools, which are used by more than half a million investors monthly and by professors and students in more than 100 universities worldwide. Dr. Tian has been featured in *Fortune*, *Forbes*, and *Barron's*. In his life prior to GuruFocus, he was a physicist and the inventor of more than 30 U.S. patents.

Index

Note: Page references followed by f indicate an illustrated figure; followed by t indicate a table.